An Internet Education

A Guide to Doing Research on the Internet

Cheryl Harris
California State University-Fullerton

An Imprint of Wadsworth Publishing Company

I(T)P® An International Thomson Publishing Company

Belmont • Albany • Bonn • Boston • Cincinnati • Detroit • London • Madrid • Melbourne
Mexico City • New York • Paris • San Francisco • Singapore • Tokyo • Toronto • Washington

Technology Editor: Kathy Shields
Assistant Editor: Tamara Huggins
Production: Ruth Cottrell
Print Buyer: Karen Hunt
Copy Editor: Ruth Cottrell
Interior Design: Image House
Cover Design: Image House
Compositor: Conch Composition
Printer: Malloy Lithographing, Inc.

Printed in the United States of America
1 2 3 4 5 6 7 8 9 10

For more information, contact Wadsworth Publishing Company.

Wadsworth Publishing Company
10 Davis Drive
Belmont, California 94002
USA

International Thomson Editores
Campos Eliseos 385, Piso 7
Col. Polanco
11560 México D. F. México

International Thomson Publishing Europe
Berkshire House 168-173
High Holborn
London, WC1V 7AA, England

International Thomson Publishing GmbH
Königswinterer Strasse 418
53227 Bonn, Germany

Thomas Nelson Australia
102 Dodds Street
South Melbourne 3205
Victoria, Australia

International Thomson Publishing Asia
221 Henderson Road
#05-10 Henderson Building
Singapore 0315

Nelson Canada
1120 Birchmount Road
Scarborough, Ontario
Canada M1K 5G4

International Thomson Publishing - Japan
Hirakawacho Kyowa Building, 3F
2-2-1 Hirakawacho
Chioda-ku, Tokyo 102, Japan

Library of Congress Cataloging-in-Publication Data

Harris, Cheryl, 1961–
     An Internet education : a guide to doing research on the Internet
  / Cheryl Harris.
     p.   cm.
     Includes bibliographical references and index.
     ISBN 0-534-25851-4
     1. Internet (Computer network)   2. Computer network resources.
3. Information services—User education. I. Title.
TK5105.875.I57H366   1995
001.4'0285'5713—dc20   95-42045

TABLE OF CONTENTS

PART 1

Introduction   1

PART 2

Conducting Research on the Internet   19

PART
3

Using Resources 65

LIST OF FIGURES

PREFACE

PURPOSE

This book is designed to introduce the process of using the Internet for research with a special emphasis on acquiring the skills needed to use Internet tools efficiently and effectively. Since the Internet is essentially chaotic — without centralized organization or control — it can be frustrating to use without a guide. This book will show you how to find and use the Internet's vast resources on demand. In addition, within the discussion of each Internet tool there is a special section that illustrates how to use the entire Internet, even if your connection is an electronic mail only one.

PREREQUISITES

In most cases, Internet applications work identically in both the Windows and Macintosh operating environments. Where there are differences, however, the author has illustrated the Windows solution. The book presumes that the user is familiar with basic computer functions such as saving files, printing files, and using dialog boxes and pull-down menus.

PROJECTS

It is strongly recommended that you reinforce your understanding of all the Internet tools through practice. Ask your instructor for research questions, follow through on issues about which you are curious, explore and "surf" the Net freely (make sure you have a firm command of "netiquette" principles before you do, however!). An excellent way to get a feel for the overall Internet is to become a regular visitor to the "What's New" sections that are part of the WWW's many site directories.

GLOSSARY/INDEX

A glossary of research and Internet-related terms is included at the end of the book as well as an index.

COMMAND AND OTHER CONVENTIONS

Commands and site addresses are separated from the text by their placement on a new line and in a different typeface. They represent examples of what you must type to communicate with your software and with other systems. The *tool* to be used (i.e., Telnet, Gopher, WWW browser, etc.) is indicated by text above the command line.

TECHNOLOGY WATCH

The Internet is a moving target — what is there today may not be there tomorrow. Already too vast to be explored in a single lifetime, it still grows at a phenomenal pace. Resources are constantly moving, being reorganized, upgraded, or replaced. For that reason, resource and site addresses have been rarely and cautiously mentioned in this text. The serious Internet student is advised to seek out one of the regularly updated directories of resources (such as Hahn's annual *The Internet Yellow Pages*, McGraw Hill), widely available at bookstores, or to routinely turn to online subject directories such as Yahoo (http://www.yahoo.com). It is wise to be prepared for change in online environments, so stay flexible and be willing to troubleshoot if resources you need are not where you expect them.

TO THE INSTRUCTOR

An online, hypertext instructor's manual with suggested projects and a comprehensive links list is available to accompany this text.

ACKNOWLEDGMENTS

Special thanks go to the following for assistance in developing this book: Kathy Shields and Tamara Huggins at Wadsworth, Ruth Cottrell (whose editorial expertise and patience are legendary), my colleagues at California State University, and the Fondation d'Art de la Napoule, France, for reminding me that offline life still exists.

1

Introduction

Someday a technology called **smart agents**[1] will patiently analyze a complete profile of our needs, our likes and dislikes, our habits, our tastes, and our exact requirements. Then we can spend time on the beach and the **agent** will do what we do not have the time or the inclination to do, such as "search every corner of the information universe."[2] Until that time, however, each of us needs to become successful and efficient in a new "information economy" that redefines our roles as essentially information workers no matter what our job title or career aspirations. Promises of unlimited leisure time have been coincident with the introduction of almost every new technological development in the twentieth century (and for the most part have not materialized), and until the halcyon days of smart agents arrive, we have our work cut out for us.

The past decade has been characterized by an explosion of information: by some estimates medical and scientific journals have increased tenfold. Every morning the average office worker is faced with a barrage of faxes, electronic mail, voice mail, Federal Express and other overnight packages and, of course, the "regular" mail. To stay current in any one field requires the expenditure of hours probably well in excess of a normal 40 hour workweek. Barry Diller, media mogul and chairman of QVC, reported recently that every morning he receives "a fat packet of at least 80 articles" from many sources, and "that has been whittled down three times before I see it."[3]

In short, we live in an information jungle. Of course we must learn to manage the jungle in order to survive, but beyond that, true expertise in information management brings with it enormous power, personal advancement, and satisfaction.

The purpose of this book is to introduce some of the powerful techniques for finding and analyzing information through the Internet. The Internet is only one of the important information resources today, and many of the techniques discussed here can also be applied to other venues.

What Is the Internet?

By late 1994 it seemed the word **Internet** was on everyone's lips. Newspapers ran front page headlines about the **information superhighway**, and in fact nearly 20,000 stories were printed in 1993–1994 using the words *information highway* or *superhighway*."[4] Giant corporations vied to cut deals that would place them in a favorable position on the infobahn. The whole concept of a new electronic culture heralded by the Internet represented the outer edge of technological promise, of rekindled hope and awe, the way space travel did in the 1960s. We are now a culture that creates and must process massive amounts of information. It is also increasingly clear that we are becoming a global culture. To survive in this environment, all of us must learn how to navigate within this new global information system—use it, manipulate it, communicate with and through it, and evolve with it. Still, in June 1994, a national Harris Poll revealed that *two-thirds* of Americans said they had not "seen, heard or read anything about the Information Superhighway."[5] Even worse, of the 34% who were aware of the topic, most claimed to have very little understanding of it.

There are good reasons for this confusion. The Internet is an entity with millions of users and millions of hosts. It has no true central organizing body or even what might be called a true organizing principle. It reaches 137 countries, and every 10 minutes a new network connects to it. In 1994, traffic on one part of the Internet, the **World Wide Web (WWW),** grew an astounding 341,634%. The breadth of the **network** is very difficult to grasp. Moreover, although the Internet offers a vast array of fascinating and useful resources, learning how to find and use the Internet's tools is difficult for most new users. There is a good reason for this because the Internet was not originally developed for the novice or even for average-skill-level computer users, but for highly skilled defense engineers and scientists who wanted a secure communications system in case of nuclear attack **(ARPAnet)** and who also needed to share remote computing resources with each other. As a result, until quite recently moving around the Internet required more than a passing knowledge of **UNIX** as well as other operating systems and command languages and quite a bit of patience.

So what is the Internet (or Net, as it is often affectionately called), really? It is by far the largest, most comprehensive collection of human knowledge and experience we have, encompassing the collections of many libraries and a myriad of other information sources. It is global in scope and exists outside many recognizable boundaries of time and place. Despite the fact that there is a large amount of unedited, unevaluated data along with the "jewels," it is an incredibly rich, diverse, and valuable tool.

Notice that I say it is a *tool*. The Net is a collection of resources with many diverting aspects—games, play areas, and all kinds of entertainment—but it is unmatched as a resource for real work and research. All Net users should be strongly warned that, if not carefully handled, the Internet is without doubt a strong promoter of procrastination. There is far too much to see and do, much of it without obvious purpose, and all of it available whenever you have a deadline to meet. Using this resource demands planning, skill, and judicious use. In addition, the Internet's amazing collection of data is more often than not unedited, and each resource must be evaluated in terms of its accuracy, validity, and reliability. This book is intended to equip new users with many of the techniques required to use the Net efficiently for research. But first, let's look at Net history and consider some of the significant future implications of the Internet.

The History of the Internet

Scientists began experimenting with linking computers to each other and to institutional sites via telephone hookups in the 1960s. This research was funded by the U.S. Defense Department's **Advanced Research Projects Agency (ARPA)**. ARPA wanted to see if computers in different locations could be connected efficiently using a new technology known as **packet switching**, which would allow several users to share one communications line. Packet switching cuts up data into discrete units, each one identified by a code or label, which can be sent over high-speed telephone lines. Each packet was given the computer equivalent of a postal address so that it could be sent to the right destination, to be reassembled shortly before reaching its destination into a message the computer could use and, finally, a human could understand.

One of the purposes of this new system, beyond allowing researchers and scientists to talk to each other, was the creation of a communications network that the government hoped would be secure in case of nuclear or other emergency. Packet switching and other protocols were designed so that if one or more **nodes** on the network went down, messages could be flexibly routed around them. The eventual development of reliable **electronic mail (E-mail)** protocols meant that even lengthy messages and files could be exchanged faster and less expensively than they could by ordinary phone calls. E-mail messages can be transmitted faster than two people can say the same things over the telephone.

As ARPA became ARPAnet (based at UCLA from 1969), users developed a way to conduct online conferences through the network. These began as discussions focusing on sciences, but eventually their scope broadened to include hundreds, and now even thousands, of subject areas. Scientists, researchers, students, professors, and government workers were attracted to these conferences as a way of exchanging information quickly and efficiently.

In the 1970s, ARPAnet split into military and civilian networks, mostly universities or defense contractors.[6] ARPA helped support the development of standards for transferring data between different types of computer networks, so that networks would reliably recognize each other and communicate. These Internet (from internetworking) protocols made it possible to develop the worldwide Internet we have today; without them, connecting to other computers would be a frustrating case of hit or miss. Within the decade, many other countries accepted the ARPAnet standards and joined the Internet. Effectively, the world was linked together via computers.

The 1980s were a time of exponential network growth. Most of this growth was in the educational sector, with thousands of colleges and universities worldwide joining the network, primarily because the National Science Foundation (overseeing the network) insisted that access be expanded and offered to as many institutions as possible. Toward the end of the decade, however, commercial organizations and large corporations began to hook their own internal networks to the Internet for worldwide access and as a way of handling messages for traveling employees. In addition to communications, hundreds of thousands of databases, files, library catalogs, and other information resources were added to the network by its participants throughout the 1980s. Access by nonuniversity or military organizations to the Internet's electronic mail and messaging systems became more widespread by 1990.

Current Status of the Internet

The Internet is at a critical turning point in its history. Just two years after policies banning commercial use were tacitly dropped, the Network has become something of a moving target, with huge gains in new users and **hosts** (**servers** that connect to the network) every month. There were times in 1994 when new users doubled every month. Today's Net is a global forum of many networks with more than 25 million users—a loose collection of millions of computers at about 500,000 sites. More than 300 gigabytes of information—the equivalent of a half-million 250 page books—flow through the system daily.

About 33% to 40% of that growth is attributed to commercial, or ".com" **domains,** a jump of 628% in just three years according to the Internet Society. Commercial use is centered on a part of the Internet known as the World Wide Web (WWW), which links together many different types of resources for improved search and retrieval and features a graphic interface with multimedia capabilities. The World Wide Web was estimated in late 1994 to have grown in excess of 356,000% in one year.[7] Nor is the growth curve over. Vinton Cerf, one of the original pioneers of the Net, believes that the Internet may soon offer more than 600 million networks (connected hosts) and be the model for the future "information superhighway."[8] By the time you read this, it is certain that the Internet will have expanded even further.

This kind of popularity does not come without a price. The frenzy to join the Internet party by businesses and hobbyists has been perceived by many long-term Net denizens as a serious threat to the cherished culture of the network, long founded on the belief that information must be freely shared, that respect for each other's privacy and opinions is paramount, and that the resources of the entire network should be used responsibly and conservatively for the greater good. In the absence of a central governing body or authority, the network ran surprisingly smoothly due to the self-governance of the Internet community. For years the Internet was arguably the only "mass media" that successfully bypassed the gatekeeping functions of the commercial press and the publishing and broadcasting industries. The large numbers of new users strain resources to their limits, and advertising efforts through the network result in intense **flame wars** (battles played through electronic mail exchanges) that in some cases bring network traffic to a near standstill. The culture clash of the experienced Internet citizens, sharing common goals and ethics, and the many "newbies," not yet "Internet socialized," is still very much underway.

Who are these new users? Demographic studies of Internet users suffer from sampling limitations due to self-selection, and they are also unable to keep up with the pace of the network's growth.[9] However, most preliminary work profiling the network's membership suggests that it is a young, affluent, and primarily male (90% by some accounts) world.[10] Although gender on the Internet is surprisingly fluid and subjective, as users shift in and out of gender roles at will in "chat forums" such as the **Internet Relay Chat (IRC)** and other discussion groups, the network has been heavily criticized for being hostile to women. Net content has also been critiqued as reflecting the interests of its peculiar demographic makeup rather than the wider audience now being attracted to it. It is said that this bias is responsible for the somewhat spotty and skewed nature of available resources.[11]

The Future of the Internet

We can speak of the Internet as being simultaneously "the new hope of the dispossessed . . . and the ultimate tool of Big Brother."[12] A networked world could be the means to the creation of a true global consciousness, bringing down the boundaries to communication that governments try to erect, but the information superhighway also has the potential to change our daily lives in ways we may not find so appealing.

Within a few years, the Internet will be part of a technological matrix in which computers, telephony, television, and other communications media have converged.[13] This highly interactive interface will provide opportunities, given enough bandwidth and computing power, to work and live in virtual spaces (environments created by **virtual reality** technology) significantly different from our experience of the world today. For some time businesses have been interested in the Internet and other new technologies as a means of dissolving or downsizing their "real space" operations in favor of their Net presence—the advertising agencies Chiat Day and Winkler McManus, the Virtual Online University, and a number of law firms come to mind as examples. Some organizations do not exist in the traditional physical sense except as the Internet links their personnel and resources together. Think tanks predict that businesses and governments will be attracted to the virtual workplace model because it allows them to reduce spending on infrastructure (buildings, equipment, etc.) and also overcomes the traditional objections to home-based workers because completely networked employees are easily monitored. This workforce would also be flexible because many, if not most, would be essentially freelancers hired on a project, contract, or seasonal basis. Moreover, virtual workers have the advantage of easy collaboration with colleagues half a world away.

True virtual reality promises to provide a seamless impression of physical presence; for example, you could experience working in an office, even seeing your office mates when you turn your head, although they are actually in Bangkok or Mogadishu—not sitting next to you.[14] On the negative side, dismantling unneeded physical infrastructure (home-based, networked workers do not need more highways, cars, office buildings, and so on) will cause the loss of many jobs.[15] The popularity of interactive, online shopping services will further contribute to the erosion of local retail economies.[16]

Even college education can be conducted online through a handful of global universities that have no actual campuses other than online forums and other meeting places. Courses could be very specific and targeted to the student's information and skill needs, and they could be given in the time frame, format, and at the pace of the individual student. Experimental workshops and courses offered online have already generated an enormous response. One such course offered through the University of Pittsburgh drew 864 people from more than 20 countries in its first term. Later this workshop attracted 19,994 students representing 54 countries.[17] Furthermore, "unlike traditional distance education systems which relied heavily on print-based materials supported by audiotape, telephone contact, videotape, color slides, study pictures, or kits containing samples, the Internet gives increased access to graphics, sound, and video files via software like **Mosaic**, as well as real-time communications. Innovative computer and telecommunication technologies expand and enhance traditional distance education by adding additional means of communication."[18] Interestingly, this educational delivery system changes the nature of student-teacher dynamics significantly: "The virtual classroom was found to be a positive yet different type of communications from the traditional classroom. This change in communication was noted by others where the experience showed that communication within a paperless network tends to spread power horizontally across the writing community, with instructor's information equal to the student's, and every message, because of identical font and identical screen size, commanding the same respect when read by a student."[19] The benefits of networked education have been described as encompassing a strengthened sense of group identity, improved dialogue, a more active learning environment, and enhanced immediacy. Nor is this potential confined to the university classroom; projects such as GREEN, Kidlink, Kidslink, the Global Schoolhouse, and Kidsphere, in which several participating countries link K–12 classrooms together, seem to have been successful.[20] Certainly the Internet's role in the future of education has far-reaching implications.[21]

The health professions have been quick to see the potential of the Internet and other new technologies, such as virtual reality, in bringing about the age of telemedicine. A recent study by Arthur D. Little concluded that advanced telecommunications could help cut the cost of health care delivery in this country by $36 billion annually through remote video doctor-patient consultations, "virtual surgery" (both for practice sessions and with remotely operated equipment for some procedures), and electronic filing of insurance claims. Not long ago, President Clinton endorsed the concept of a universal patient information identity card that would have an individual's entire medical history encoded on it. It could be swiped into a networked information system during a visit to a doctor or a hospital. However, the idea was quickly dropped because of consumer outrage. Still, many believe the medical identity card will be adopted in the future.

Shopping online is already in development, awaiting the release of a secure **encryption** scheme. In the absence of such a scheme, many businesses that are already online are taking orders with credit cards that are faxed or even E-mailed by buyers browsing commercial WWW sites. Everything from books and flowers to cruises—even furniture and jewelry—are there now.

The economic and social impact of these events will be considerable. The North America of the virtual information worker will be one in which physical isolation is common, with travel becoming more expensive, so that face-to-face contact and other personal services will probably be reserved for the wealthy.[22] The potential of constant surveillance of almost every aspect of our lives (our work output, our communications with others, our purchase and travel patterns, our tastes and preferences, etc.) will all be available for scrutiny by any authority with the software and access to bring together the appropriate databases.[23] Several major corporations are now pursuing the development of software that would scour the networks to bring together consumer information in one massive marketing super-database. At a National Research Council conference in Washington, D.C. in 1993, Representative Edward Markey noted that "new marketing technologies are being refined using sophisticated software that takes huge amounts of information collected from various sources and combine it into a single database."[24] This powerful cross-referenced information has been dubbed "recombinant information."[25] This information can include court records, credit card balances, bank account information, magazine subscriptions, store purchases, and other personal data collected by companies of all kinds and aggressively marketed to anyone willing to pay for it.[26] The Internet, of course, promises unparalleled ease in pulling together multiple data sources.

The trail of purchase transaction-related data is not the only problem. Now one can walk into a library, pull books off a shelf, look at them, and leave. However, Internet online libraries track all access behavior and store it for future use. Knowledge monitoring could be just as problematic in its consequences as someone knowing where you shop and what you buy. What is certain is that public policy, law, and regulation are far behind the potential of new electronic technologies like the Internet to easily assemble and distribute information.[27]

Information security and who will have access to "private" information are not only consumer concerns. The U.S. government has vigorously pushed to implement the **Clipper Chip** technology, which would allow it access to encryption keys for any communication—public or private—in the country, ostensibly to prevent criminal use of the network and to protect government data.[28] Clipper Chip has been the center of intense controversy among the Internet communities and elsewhere because the U.S. government's vision allows it the ability to crack any code, but top-level decryption would not be shared with other governments or with private companies. In other words, a Clipper Chip built into every U.S. computer (and other electronic goods, such as telephones and fax machines) would probably face serious export problems and would interfere with global communications because no other government would willingly agree to let the United States have access to its communications if it did not have access to the communications of the United States. Right now, the potential for international and industrial espionage by monitoring commercial and government traffic on the Internet is enormous.[29]

On the other hand, the Internet has already shown its immense power for democratization and grassroots mobilization.[30] The kind of direct access to information that the Internet offers is seen by some as "inherently politically subversive."[31] When China blocked all other communication channels during the Tienanmen Square debacle, university students sent hour-by-hour updates around the world via a hastily rigged Internet connection. Because most of our current political structures are territorially based but the Internet is not, the resulting virtual community with its decentralized power could produce governance of a different order.[32] There is fear that the forum the Internet offers for political debate could be one where little real discussion occurs beyond the visceral and superficial, with instant decision making or voting possible . . . not at all what Thomas Jefferson had in mind when he visualized "thinking individuals self-actualizing a democracy."[33] Markey, in his address to other government officials, asked: "Will cyberspace become some lawless place, where the Constitution is cracked open by fiber fissures created when trying to convert a two hundred year old parchment into a binary world of zeros and 1's? Can [the Constitution] continue to be a 'living, breathing document' in such an environment? Or will cyberspace develop its own distinct laws? Will it develop 'digital vigilantes' to patrol and police the electronic bulletin boards and electronic highways? What indigenous political institutions may develop in such a vacuum?"[34]

The second half of the twentieth century has in general been marked by a worldwide "obsolescence of hierarchical, command institutions," such as the abrupt collapse of the Soviet Union. A report on "Society, Cyberspace and the Future" sponsored by the Markle Foundation and the Aspen Society asserted that the "prevailing global trend is now strongly toward dispersion of authority and responsibility downward and outward." Horizontal political structures, relationships, markets, and organizations will probably be the result of widespread use of the Internet in the "Post-Command Era."[35]

Perhaps the most serious and immediate issues have to do with decisions about whether or not steps will be taken to distribute access to the network to less advantaged classes. Open access in the public interest is the focus of the Clinton administration's Open Platform Initiative, included in several bills related to the National Communications Information Infrastructure Act (NII),[36] although the outcome of this legislation is still in doubt at of the time of this writing. Paying for true "open access" would be incredibly costly and would require a substantial federal subsidy or, as Richard Sclove of the Loka Institute—a think tank devoted to new technology issues—suggested, a new tax. "Pay for access through a tax on commercial use of the Internet" and use these dollars locally for access and to compensate for "damages to civic life" that the "information superhighway" will bring.[37] Left to the devices of the marketplace, it is certain that disadvantaged households will suffer.[38] Households in which the adults earn "$50,000 a year or more and at least one adult has a college education are five times more likely to own a PC now and ten times more likely to go online." Children without access to PCs at home "cannot compete on an equal basis with those who do. . . ." Experts agree that "if the road to equality is access to information technology, then there are already significant roadblocks in place."[39] Access to computers currently splits along ethnic lines as well as by income and education, with whites three times more likely to own home computers and to use them at work than other ethnic groups. The "90s populist slogan is no longer 'a chicken in every pot' but 'a computer on every desk'."[40] In the age of information overload, computer fluency will not be optional. "We're growing into a culture which is global and deals with massive amounts of information. It's not enough to try and memorize it all . . . you have to learn how to find it, use it, manipulate it and communicate with it."[41]

If we have learned anything from our past experiences with innovation and its unintended consequences, we will welcome public scrutiny of and participation in its development. Because the information superhighway figures prominently in so many plans for the future, it is certain that whatever decisions are made now will influence our lives well into the twenty-first century.[42]

Implications of the Internet for You

Researchers agree that income differences will probably widen as the economy evolves, "pitting Americans with less education against computerized machines and people in low wage nations, such as China. . . ."[43] Computer fluency will be such a valued aspect of education that it is expected to add as much as several hundred thousand dollars to salary expectations over an average working life, and fluency will be a function of one's ability to use networked systems such as the Internet to locate, retrieve, and analyze widely dispersed information resources.[44] Businesses are currently committing millions of dollars to evaluating or building an Internet presence, and they will undoubtedly seek future employees who are comfortable with that environment.[45] Lawrence Wilkinson of the Global Business Network says that ". . . there's not a business that will not be remade by the Internet by the turn of the century, or just thereafter," and many will in fact become "virtual companies," with flatter hierarchies and a dependence on a highly trained and educated workforce.[46] In the next decade, most of the economic growth is expected to occur in the proliferation of small businesses, and they are going to have the most to gain from an Internet presence. They will be aggressively looking for recruits who bring excellent Internet research skills with them. Large companies will also use the Internet extensively, but mostly for customer care and service. All will use the Internet for information. Already there is evidence that marketing through the WWW is perhaps four times less expensive and potentially more effective than marketing through traditional channels.[47] As if that were not enough reason to enhance one's market competitiveness through acquiring the proper skills, it is also considered likely that the largely unmetered nature of Internet information access will change into a system more similar to an "information tollway," where each bit of information will be available for a price. Efficiency and high productivity will be essential to keep information costs down.

In the short run, the Internet can be of immense benefit to you in all kinds of different areas, such as research for class assignments, job hunting, communications, and other activities. The Internet offers a more convenient, less time consuming and expensive way of performing these tasks in many cases. For example, if you need to pull together the most recent data on lung cancer mortality rates in a certain area, as well as interview experts on the disease, the Internet can make this a viable project over the course of just a few days or hours, whereas it might otherwise have taken you several weeks (if you could even get access to the experts through traditional channels). Perhaps you need to find a summer internship in London. The Internet can bring you a database of contacts and job openings throughout the world, frequently updated, that otherwise would have been almost impossible to find. Or you might, as I do, have friends in other parts of the world with whom you would like to keep in touch regularly. The Internet provides an excellent and inexpensive way to do all of these tasks.

The bottom line is that in the foreseeable future, Internet literacy will be rewarded by the marketplace and will be a considerable asset; it will be well worth the trouble of developing a proficiency in all of the basic areas covered in this book.

Network Ethics

A complete discussion of network etiquette, or "Netiquette," is contained in the next chapter. However, a few ground rules are in order before we begin. Remember that the Internet is often spoken of as a community, with its own culture (and subcultures). Members of this culture are famously helpful but equally as intolerant of obvious boorishness. Because the communications tools of the Internet, electronic mail, and the forums are so immediate and casual in nature, it is easy to toss off messages without considering what you say. Avoid this temptation and think through your messages before hitting the Send button. All of the behaviors that are disapproved of in face-to-face social interactions, such as gossiping, lying, harassment, lack of consideration for others, and so on, are regarded just as unfavorably online.

It is easy to forget that hackers, which is the term applied to those who are computer savvy and whose joy in life is doing things with computers (different from **crackers**, which is the proper term for those who break into computers, steal information, or otherwise use the Network for illegal or criminal activity), built the Internet. Much of the software, theory, and ideas that run the Net were produced, not by people who were being paid big salaries by major corporations to develop them but by Internet citizens who did it for the fun of it. Honor this spirit of innovation. Realize when you run into a bug or a site "under construction" that IBM, Microsoft, and AT&T do not run the Internet kingdom . . . yet. Accept that the Internet is growing rapidly and will continue to evolve and change. It takes a certain flexibility to adapt to this constantly changing environment, but this quality is as much a part of succeeding in the Information Age as knowing which buttons to push.

Probably the best advice is: "Be conservative in what you send; be generous in what you accept."[48] This statement has several layers of meaning, the most obvious of which is that instant and cheap communications media invite misuse through over-messaging. You will probably receive more than you would like, but it is not a good idea to return the favor.

Privacy

Privacy, as it pertains to the Internet, is a tangled issue because realistically one's identity cannot be effectively masked. Everywhere you travel through the Internet, every action you take, leaves a **digital vapor trail** that can usually be easily traced. Even "anonymous remailer" services, which intercept your message and strip out the identifying headers, will probably soon be challenged in the courts so that crime over the Internet cannot hide behind them. Electronic mail has already been the target of several legal battles, some of which establish the precedent that electronic mail is *not* private and can be read by employers, for example. For this reason, err on the side of reason, good sense, and decency when communicating through the Net.

In addition, individual domains as well as the major Internet advisory bodies have developed policies and procedures for Internet usage to which they expect all users to adhere. Known as **acceptable use policies (AUPs)**, these policy statements specify rules for determining, for example, what will be considered business use and what will be considered personal use of network resources; consequences for disrupting network traffic or crashing a network or its connected systems; unauthorized access issues; theft of data, equipment, or intellectual property; and so on. At a minimum, failing to observe acceptable use policies will result in flames (unpleasant messages from disapproving users), suspension of computer privileges, or even legal action. Make certain you know and can comply with all AUP agreements at your institution or company as well as the Internet-wide AUPs.[49]

Purpose of This Book and How to Use It

This book is designed to introduce the process of using the Internet for research as well as the skills needed to use the Internet's various tools efficiently. Both research design and data analysis are stressed because good planning is essential to productive search and retrieval strategies and other forms of research through the Net, and superior data analysis skills are required when so *much of the Internet's data is unedited, sometimes uncredited, and under no centralized control.* However, there is no substitute for learning by doing—getting on the network and trying out what you have learned. Do not be discouraged by experienced users who will tell you it's easy. Most of us who have been working with the Internet for a long time were self-taught before there was any documentation of the system or even easily available guides to UNIX, the operating system run by most host computers connected to the Internet. For example, I learned about the Internet on mainframe computers using dumb **terminals** in the mid 1980s, using arcane command language and connecting to other hosts on a trial-and-error basis. **Graphical user interfaces (GUIs)**, point-and-click **hypertext** applications, and the other wonders of present-day Internet access are new developments. In retrospect, after 10 years of experience, it's easy for me to think that most things about the Internet are reasonably logical and straightforward. Yet I have taught enough new users how to get around to be aware that it is still full of sufficient anachronisms and clunky idiosyncrasies to create significant user frustration. I hope I have succeeded in convincing you that it is worth the effort, however. Use this guide to get started, learn by doing, and step into the Information Age.

Endnotes

1. Words printed in boldface are keywords that appear in the glossary.

2. Diller, B. (1995, February). Don't Repackage, Redefine. *Wired,* pp. 82–84.

3. Ibid.

4. Reality Check. (1994, July/August). *Aldus Magazine,* p. 47.

5. Singer, M. (1994, June 15). Superhighway a Mystery to Most. *Folio: The Magazine for Magazine Management,* p. 20.

6. Temer, E. (1994, Summer). Learning from the Net. *Wilson Quarterly,* pp. 18–28.

7. WWW Closes in on Top-Ranked Service. (1995, February 1). *The Internet Letter: On Corporate Users, Internetworking and Information Services,* p. 5.

8. Ubois, J. (1994, September). Present at the Creation. *Internet World,* pp. 66–69.

9. Harris, C. (1995, Fall, forthcoming). Survey Research and the Internet. *Electronic Journal* of *Virtual Culture.* (http://www.marshall.edu./vstepp/vri/ejvc/ejvc.html); Humphrey, D. (1995, March). Online Industry Research. *Online Access,* p. 32.

10. Industry Byte. (1995, March). *Online Access,* p. 17; Aware, the Boys Are. (1995, March). *NetGuide,* p. 25. WWW Site with demographics; result of survey.

11. Edwards, H. C. (1994, July/August). Geting Wired. *Aldus Magazine,* pp. 36–39.

12. Strangelove, M. (1994, July 21). The Geography of Consciousness. *Research on Virtual Culture.* (http://www.phoenix.ca/sie/geo-art.html)

13. Trends & Interfaces. (1994, November). *PC World,* p. 182.

14. Gold, J. (1994, May 1). Working It Out. *Los Angeles Times Magazine,* p. 10.

15. Maddox, T. (1994, Summer). The Cultural Consequences of the Information Superhighway. *Wilson Quarterly,* pp. 29–36.

16. Sclove, R. (1994, June 2). The Social Effects of the Internet. *Internet World.* Conference paper.

17. Smith, R. J. (1991, October). The Electronic Information Course as an Alternative Teaching Method. *Research and Education Networking,* pp. 10–12.

18. Ibid.

19. Ibid.

20. Taylor, R. (1994, September). Brave New Internet. *Internet World,* pp. 36–42.

21. Blystone, K. (1993, August 20). Building a School without Buildings. *Electronic Journal of Virtual Culture.*

22. Gans, H. J. (1994, Winter). The Electronic Shut-ins: Some Social Flaws of the Information Superhighway. *Media Studies Journal,* pp. 123–129.

23. Rosentiel, T. B. (1994, May 18). Someone May Be Watching. *Los Angeles Times,* p. A12.

24. Markey, E. J. (1993, February 18). Networked Communities and the Laws of Cyberspace. In *Computer Science and Telecommunications Board. Rights and Responsibilities of Participants in Networked Communities.* Washington, DC: National Research Council/Academy of Sciences.

25. Larsen, E. (1994). *The Naked Consumer: How Our Private Lives Become Public Commodities.* Penguin Books.

26. Larsen, E. (1994). *The Naked Consumer: How Our Private Lives Become Public Commodities.* Penguin Books; Markey, E. J. (1993, February 18). Networked Communities and the Laws of Cyberspace. In *Computer Science and Telecommunications Board. Rights and Responsibilities of Participants in Networked Communities.* Washington, DC: National Research Council/Academy of Sciences.

27. Rothfeder, J. (1992). *Privacy for Sale: How Computerization Has Made Everyone's Private Life an Open Secret.* Simon & Schuster.

28. Meeks, B. (1994, February 9). The End of Privacy. *Wired,* p. 18; Barlow, J. P. (1994, February 9). Jackboots on the Infobahn. *Wired;* Godwin, M. (1994, June). Libel, Public Figures, and The Net. *Internet World,* pp. 62–64; Ventura, M. (1994, May 8). The 21st Century Is Now. *Los Angeles Times Magazine,* pp. 22–26.

29. Godwin, M. (1994, September). Government Eavesdropping. *Internet World,* pp. 93–95.

30. Keighron, P. (1994, June 10). Superhighway Robbery: Social and Economic Impact of the Information Superhighway. *New Statesman & Society,* p. 31.

31. Wright, R. (1994, January/February). Life on the Internet. *Utne Reader,* pp. 101–109.

32. Wright, R. (1994, January/February). Life on the Internet. *Utne Reader,* pp. 101–109; Strangelove, M. (1994, July 21). The Geography of Consciousness. *Research on Virtual Culture;* Taylor, R. (1994, September). Brave New Internet. *Internet World,* pp. 36–42.

33. Sclove, R. E. (1994, January 12). Democratizing Technology. *The Chronicle of Higher Education,* p. B1.

34. Markey, E. J. (1993, February 18). Networked Communities and the Laws of Cyberspace. In *Computer Science and Telecommunications Board. Rights and Responsibilities of Participants in Networked Communities.* Washington, DC: National Research Council/Academy of Sciences.

35. Murray, B. (1995, February). Society, Cyberspace and the Future. Aspen Exploratory Workshop. The Markle Foundation; Gilliam, D. (1994, March 19). Getting on Today's Road to Freedom. *The Washington Post,* p. B1.

36. Karraker, R. (1994, Spring). Making Sense of the "Information Superhighway." *Whole Earth Review,* pp. 18–24.

37. Sclove, R. (1994, June 2). The Social Effects of the Internet. *Internet World.* Conference paper.

38. Farhi, P. (1993, December 19). Will the Information Superhighway Detour the Poor? *The Washington Post,* p. H1.

39. Furger, R. (1994, September). Unequal Distribution: The Information Haves and Have-Nots. *PC World,* p. 30.

40. Hancock, L. (1995, February 27). The Haves and the Have Nots. *Newsweek,* pp. 50–53.

41. Digital Connections: Kids and the Future. (1994, November). *Medea Magazine,* p. 40.

42. Sclove, R. E. (1994, January 12). Democratizing Technology. *The Chronicle of Higher Education,* p. B1; Sclove, R., & Scheur, J. (1994, May 29). The Ghost in the Modem. *The Washington Post,* p. E2.

43. Arndt, M. (1994, July 22). Census: College Cost Is High; So Is Payoff. *San Diego Union Tribune,* pp. Al & A10.

44. Ibid.

45. Matarazzo, J., & Manshel, D. (1994, March 30). Info-highway to Nowhere. *Christian Science Monitor,* p. 22.

46. Herbert, J. (1995, March). Mega Connections and Other Questions. *Medea Magazine,* pp. 18–19.

47. Novak, D. (1995, January 1). Challenges of Electronic Commerce. *Wired,* p. 17.

48. Deutsch, P. (1994, September). The Ten Commandments of the Internet. *Internet World,* pp. 96–98.

49. Seabrok, J. (1994, June 6). Brave New World Dept. My First Flame. *The New Yorker,* pp. 70–79; Saunders, L. (1994, June 2). Ethics in Cyberspace. *Internet World.* Conference paper; Nickell, N. (1994). Internet Users "Lock Up" Lawyers for Breach of "Netiquette." *The Arizona Republic,* p. D1.

2

Conducting Research on the Internet

Getting and Using an Internet Connection

At the time of publication of this book, most university campuses offered student and faculty accounts free of charge or for a nominal fee, but these accounts are primarily shell accounts as opposed to the **SLIP** (Serial Line Interface Protocol) or **PPP** (Point-to-Point Protocol) accounts that commercial access providers emphasize. Shell or dial-up accounts cannot take advantage of the **graphical user interface (GUI)** and point-and-click capabilities of the Windows™ and Macintosh™ environments. These accounts also depend on the user having at least a minimal familiarity with basic **UNIX** operating system commands in order to navigate, and they have the disadvantage of requiring an extra step in order to get documents or files from the original location to the server and then to your computer's hard drive. Shell accounts treat the user's PC as a **terminal** on the system and so there are sometimes terminal emulation problems. Ask your system administrator if you can get a SLIP/PPP connection as a first preference, but if a dial-up account is your only way to connect, all is not lost. However, you may eventually want to pay for a SLIP account through a commercial provider for enhanced ease of use.

FIGURE 1   AN EXAMPLE OF A SHELL ACCOUNT INTERFACE ON A UNIX SYSTEM

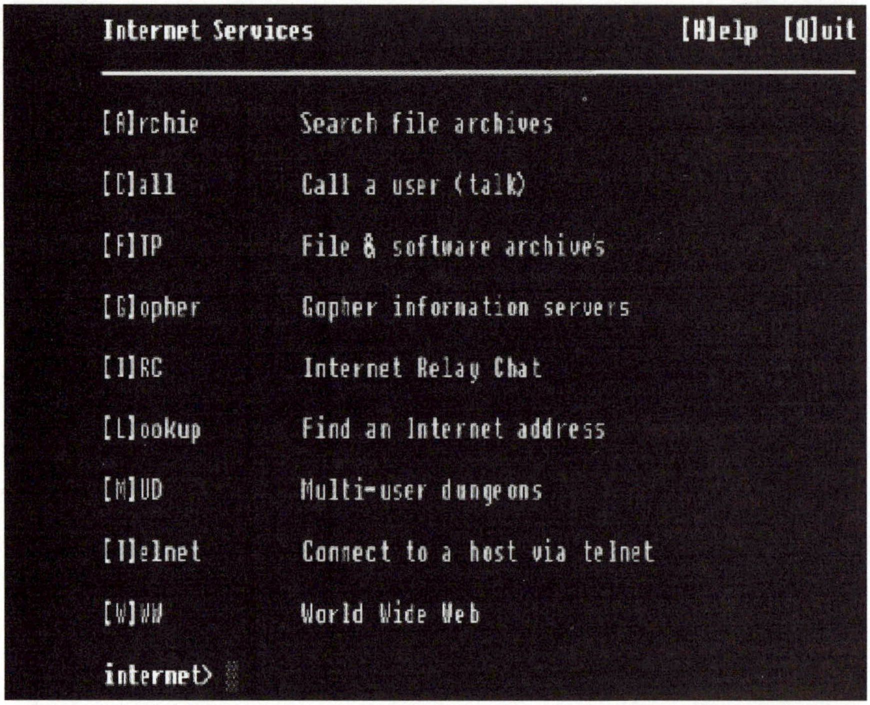

```
Internet Services                               [H]elp [Q]uit
_____

   [A]rchie        Search file archives

   [C]all          Call a user (talk)

   [F]TP           File & software archives

   [G]opher        Gopher information servers

   [I]RC           Internet Relay Chat

   [L]ookup        Find an Internet address

   [M]UD           Multi-user dungeons

   [T]elnet        Connect to a host via telnet

   [W]WW           World Wide Web

internet>
```

The cost of a basic individual account varies considerably depending on geographic location. Some providers charge as little as $10 a month for service, while others charge much more. Shop around before committing to a commercial service because some charge for each minute or hour of connect time, which can prove very expensive while you are a novice. As you become more efficient, trade in your shell account if you can and become a "node" on the Net, which essentially gives you the advantages of a SLIP/PPP account. Although commercial services such as Prodigy, Compuserve, and America Online all planned (or had already implemented) Internet-wide E-mail and WWW access as of April 1995, these services are typically more expensive than a full-service local Internet access provider. Make sure you compare annual service costs, including hourly fees. Be generous when estimating the number of hours you will be online; most Internet users find that as their proficiency grows, so does the amount of time they are online.

Acceptable Use Policies

No matter which type of connection you arrange, the service provider will ask you to agree to certain policies and procedures before finalizing your account. Read these statements carefully and completely and be certain you understand the responsibilities and privileges attached to your account. Ask for documentation from the support staff about the system you will be using; log-in procedures, file storage limits, available gateways to Internet resources, text editors, E-mail front ends, and so on are unique to each system. You may need training on basic UNIX commands (similar to DOS in many cases, but more powerful) if you are using a shell account. If you are fortunate enough to have a SLIP/PPP or direct Internet connection, you may need help configuring the software so it can run correctly on your system. It is in your best interests to begin building a friendly and courteous relationship with the technical support staff attached to your server system. *Do* ask them for guidance when you have technical problems associated with your system configuration and connection. *Do not* barrage technical support staff with demands for pointers to Internet resources (such as "How do I find a GIF called . . . ?") because this is not their function and will quickly cause an already overwhelmed technical staff to ignore your pleas for help. Use this book, current Internet directories, and other research techniques to find specific resources. Save tech support's goodwill for when you *really* need it.

The Logic of Internet Structure

One of the primary reasons this book was written is that the Internet was designed by technically sophisticated computer engineers and scientists for their own use. They never anticipated the huge wave of inexperienced computer users now interested in the Internet. Moreover, most of the mainframe servers or nodes on the network are administered by equally sophisticated computer experts whose language of choice is really UNIX—not English, French, or Swahili. This is the reason that much of the Internet's structure seems unfamiliar to new users. PC users enjoy a slight advantage when moving through Internet space for the first time because the organization of files into directories and subdirectories with truncated names is somewhat similar to that used by Microsoft's DOS. Macintosh users who are used to a file organization system of folders and icons will find the UNIX file structure awkward and unfamiliar. However, UNIX, while strange to most of us, can be learned. Just a few commands and a basic knowledge of file structure will be enough to get you around. You will not need to do elaborate programming.

Typically, your account will provide access to the Internet from a UNIX server where you are given a workspace with specific limits. This workspace is where you end up when you log in. Your E-mail address will reflect the identity and perhaps the physical location of this server. For example, my E-mail address *charris@ccvax.fullerton.edu* indicates that my workspace is located on CCVAX (one of several servers at my university); FULLERTON is the university name (California State University, Fullerton), and EDU reveals that my **domain** type is an educational institution. Domains are important clues about the affiliation or origin of information on the Net and will be discussed further in the section on electronic mail.

UNIX systems store virtually everything in a file, but files may contain different types of information. A file may include a program source code, text files, software, photographs, sound clips, and images. Files are stored within a directory (that may in turn be nested within other directories, when it then becomes a subdirectory). UNIX commands are used to navigate through this directory and file system and to run specific programs (such as **Telnet**) to connect to another server and look at its files. You must understand this file structure because UNIX can locate files only with a reference to the complete path statement. A path is the location of a file by server, directory, subdirectories (if applicable), and file name. Conceptually, a path is much like a tree, with branches representing routes to files. To run a program or read a file you must move to the directory that actually contains it, or you must include its full path address in the command that loads or runs it.

Common UNIX Commands

A few basic commands will get you around in your workspace in a shell account. The following commands that are specific to Internet functions will be discussed in the appropriate section later in this book.

UNIX Command	What It Does
cd	moves to another directory (stands for "change directory," i.e., cd mydirectory)
cdup	moves upward to the directory above the one you're in
ls	lists the contents of a directory
dir	lists the contents of a directory (on some but not all UNIX servers)
mkdir	creates a new directory
rmdir	removes a directory (generally must be empty first)
del	deletes a file; requires file name to be specified
pwd	shows current directory name (the one you are in)
help	executes a help file on your local system; accesses local documentation
man	executes a help file on your local system; accesses local documentation

Again, make sure you receive current log-in instructions (from campus, home, or office locations) and anything else that pertains to your specific account and server from your system administrator. Count on spending at least a day or two familiarizing yourself with your local server environment and your account workspace before moving on to the rest of the Internet.

Research Basics

Once you develop a familiarity with the basic navigational tools, one of the challenges you will face in your Internet experience will be finding the specific information and resources you want scattered among its millions of servers. More important than simply finding information will be determining the validity and reliability of that information and how it may be applied to your original research problem or question. In other words, it is not enough just to **surf** the Net and come across interesting sites and files almost by accident. To realize the full potential of the Internet, you must learn how to bring a disciplined and focused set of research skills to it. Only then does the Internet cease being a novelty or toy and become a true resource for *real work*.

Information needs are increasingly a part of our daily lives: to plan a work-study tour in Tunisia, you need to develop local contacts and gather pertinent facts about the area; to write a term paper for a political science class, you may need to find transcripts of the president's speeches and White House press releases. Work as a nurse may lead to questions about new patient care philosophies; a marketer seeking to determine the feasibility of introducing a new product may need new ways of assessing potential market interest; and so on. Whether you are a student, a teacher, an entrepreneur, or a business person, you need a constant stream of information to function in your role. The problem we have today is not a scarcity of information; it is information *overload*. Organizing, evaluating, and making sense of massive amounts of information is now a real job description for many of us. To do it well, we must have access to a set of tools that will allow us to perform these tasks efficiently and productively.

Research methodologies are essentially tools that provide different ways of structuring information, from the design of a research question to the analysis stage. Each method has a different potential outcome, and the pros and cons associated with each choice must be weighed against what you hope to accomplish. Good research skills contribute greatly to the efficiency of your work. Proper research procedures will also help ensure that the information you use to make decisions is reliable and useful.

Research Goals

Research is a process. Typically, it involves numerous steps and many decisions along the way, beginning with the selection of a topic or problem. Often, the selection of a topic must be followed by a thorough review of existing literature or databases to determine what is already known. This is advisable (1) to avoid repeating a study when information is already available and (2) to suggest an informed and appropriate theoretical or conceptual approach. The Internet is one of the most valuable resources for this step because of the large number of online libraries and publications, easily searchable and often available 24 hours a day. If facilitating the literature review were the only advantage that the Internet offered, it would still be significant. It is possible to do a comprehensive keyword search in an online catalog such as CARL/UNCOVER, for example, and in a few moments you can have the full text of an article faxed, E-mailed, or downloaded for use.

Perhaps the most important step in the research process is the development of the research question or questions. How you phrase your overall research goal and specific objectives will have a great impact on the outcome. What tools will be appropriate to address it, what you will count as data, and how you will evaluate the information you find are all factors that have a direct bearing on the research question itself. It is essential to develop as focused and realistic a research question as possible.

Only after the research question has been clarified and refined can you decide which tool from the toolbox is best for your purpose. The selection of a methodology and the overall plan (your research design) will usually be suggested by the nature of your research question. Some research questions, for example, will require long-term qualitative approaches, such as in-depth interviews. Others will lead you to different methods. How to select an appropriate tool will be discussed in detail later.

Using the Internet to collect data or information is facilitated by doing the research design preparation first so that once you go online, all you need to do is move to the area of the Internet that is likely to hold the information you need, doing the appropriate searches (preferably with one of the fast-search engines we'll soon discuss) and downloading what you need to be analyzed later. Finally, data analysis and presentation of results are closely related to the nature of the research method used.

Remember that the overall goal of good research is to be as comprehensive as possible *within the boundaries of your research question*. This includes developing an appropriate context for the work (the purpose of a literature review), collecting targeted data, and finding meaningful patterns in the information you discover.

Areas of the Internet for Research

The Internet can be conceptualized as consisting of various services or areas, each of which provides different opportunities for research. Brief descriptions of these areas follow.

DATABASES

Thousands of databases are accessible via the Internet, with statistics on virtually everything imaginable. These include extensive government census data archives, airline schedules, traffic reports, weather reports, and even minute-by-minute stock market data. The Internet connects databases scattered all over the world, some of which are not accessible except to Internet users. There are also huge archives of free and low-cost software that researchers will find useful.

LIBRARIES

Formerly, people doing certain kinds of archival research inevitably ended up on planes traveling to far-flung, dusty library stacks. Today, many, if not most, major metropolitan, government, and university libraries have online catalogs (often referred to as PACs or OPACs, for Public Access Catalog or Online Public Access Catalog), and an amazing number are accessible via Internet connections. Some libraries are now moving aggressively to put their collections online, particularly the kinds of rare archival materials that used to require travel. In addition, over the past decade many libraries have moved in the direction of sharing their resources rather than duplicating them. This is far more cost-effective, and the benefit for us is that many journals, newspapers, and books exist online to facilitate exchange. Exploring distant resources as though you were on site is one of the wonders of the Internet.

USENET: DISCUSSION GROUPS

Frequently, research requires quickly locating a group of people involved in a certain issue or problem. The Usenet is a collection of thousands of discussion groups on every imaginable topic. It is extremely niched, and as such it has important implications for locating experts; doing ethnographic research; conducting certain kinds of interviews; and gathering facts, anecdotes, and stories in a very focused, targeted way.

E-MAIL AND LISTSERVS

Like the Usenet, tools such as electronic mail and Listservs (by-subscription-only discussion groups) are powerful ways to connect to experts and others who can assist you in your research.

REMOTE COMPUTING RESOURCES

Researchers working with large datasets sometimes need access to more powerful computers, more storage space, or other computing resources. The Internet offers a number of ways to use remote computing resources, such as supercomputers, that would otherwise not be available to researchers.

Weaknesses of the Internet for Research

While information and data are abundant throughout the Internet (more than 30,000 times more data is on the Internet than in the Library of Congress), it is premature to claim that anything you might want to know is available there. For one thing, the Internet lacks a comprehensive catalog of its reference materials. Also, because resources have been added voluntarily to the public Internet servers by individuals and organizations throughout the world, information may appear to be very deep in one area but superficial or missing in others, depending on the needs and interests of the users who put the materials online. However, because the network grows by leaps and bounds each day, it is difficult to state categorically that the Internet is weak in specific areas because tomorrow it may not be. Still, I find that the Internet should be used cautiously when research questions involve:

1. *Finding historical information on any subject prior to about 1990.* Although the Library of Congress catalog, listing all books published in the United States since the establishment of the Library, can be accessed via its WWW site, and for a fee practically any article can be delivered to you by the CARL/UNCOVER system, there are still few online resources for electronic texts going back more than a couple of years. Commercial database services and print materials are better comprehensive resources for historical research, although there are Internet sites that supplement these with unique offerings. For example, just last week a classics professor announced a new site titled "The Eighteenth Century WWW," with a surprising collection of digitized texts, art, and scholarly articles and rumors of more to come.

2. *Information about privately held or small companies.* Numerous and extensive resources on the Internet provide research, statistics, and profiles on publicly held companies, ranging from the Thomas Register of Manufacturers to the research reports issued by the major brokerage firms and, of course, the WWW pages maintained by the companies themselves that tell you all about their firms. Well over half of all U.S. companies with sales above $1 billion currently have a WWW presence. Although small and private companies are adding their own WWW homepages, which may be good sources of information about their structures and philosophies, it may be difficult to research them in depth via the Internet.

3. *Dictionaries or business handbooks for specific industries.* These resources are so far available for many foreign-trade,

import-export businesses, but other industries have yet to follow their lead.

4. *Small, specialized commercial database suppliers.* Lexis-Nexus, Dialog, Dow Jones News Service, Nielsen, and other large database suppliers have long had a Net presence, often slashing their rates for Internet customers. Thousands of smaller commercial database companies are still not on the Net, but it is likely that over the next 18 to 24 months many will make the move. Interestingly, many commercial services that are available via proprietary dial-up connections or CD-ROM for hefty fees are available without charge on the Internet, including up-to-the-minute U.S. patent filings and SEC releases. Commercial database suppliers will probably join the Internet en masse when per-use payment schemes permitting secure encrypted transactions become available.

5. *Information about companies headquartered outside the United States.* Asia, Europe, and Latin America experienced a steep growth curve in the number of servers joining the Internet in 1994. As more non-U.S. companies add their networks to the Internet, it will become easier to perform competitive intelligence and basic research concerning companies in other countries.

6. *Local court reports and other judicial/legal information.* Several courts at the state level have begun putting their court records online (a rich resource for legal researchers as well as aspiring crime writers), but few lower courts are now online. However, many local jurisdictions do routinely put their reports on city bulletin board systems (BBSs), which can be dialed directly.

7. *Telephone directories.* Although available on CD-ROM, searchable databases of residential and telephone directories have not gone online, with the exception of the U.K. Yellow Pages and the recent Internet Phone Directory, a list of users of a new software product that allows people to make domestic and international phone calls through the Internet for the cost of a local call. However, in late April 1995 American Business Information (ABI) announced a venture to put its database of 11 million U.S. businesses online sometime before the end of the year.[1]

8. *Biographies of executives and celebrities.* While biographies of VIPs are sometimes available at a company's WWW site or as part of a star's fan club homepage, there is not yet an organized single, reliable source similar to the print version of "Who's Who. . . ." A "Who's Who on the Internet" directory does exist, but it is not moderated. Anyone can add himself or herself to it. Before

using a biography or other factual data, be sure to evaluate its source!

9. *Business or marketing information in languages other than English.* So far, much of the business reference material has been made available in English. Although many Usenet groups are conducted in languages other than English, most public databases are in English. It is difficult to say how soon non-English information sources will begin to be common.

Research Methods

The cost of information is dropping to the point where experts predict that soon most basic information will be free (perhaps this is why leading commercial database suppliers are so willing to cut prices when they go online). However, custom research and intelligent analysis will be costly. A good working knowledge of the research process and basic methods is essential for success.

THE IMPORTANCE OF CHOOSING THE RIGHT TOOL

Research methods are like camera lenses; you carry several lenses in your camera bag, but you don't use them all at once or even interchangeably. You quickly learn that if you choose to use the zoom lens, you must give up a considerable amount of *context* in the resulting photograph. Likewise, if you use a wide-angle lens, you sacrifice detail. So it is with choosing a research tool; different methods yield different results. The savvy researcher thinks long and hard about the relationship of the project's objectives and the possible results before choosing a method of approach or *tool*, because the choice of that tool will be intimately related to the findings. The bottom line is that each of the common research tools has specific advantages and disadvantages that must be considered before an educated choice can be made. With respect to the Internet, the normal trade-offs become a bit more complicated because there are additional challenges involved when doing research through the Internet. The pros and cons associated with various approaches will be discussed later in this chapter.

SOURCES OF ERROR IN RESEARCH

The process of seeking answers to questions is always subject to errors that are often outside the researcher's control. While we cannot always eliminate research errors, we can take steps to minimize them.

Research errors can include:

1. Bias in selecting a research question or failure to formulate a researchable question.

2. Selection of an inappropriate sampling method, lack of rigor in sample selection, or selection of a sample from an incomplete or poor list.

3. Construction of an inappropriate measurement instrument: interview questions, questionnaires, protocols, content analytic categories, etc.

4. Interviewer error or bias.

5. Data analysis error (data entry problems, wrong statistical tests, data incorrectly interpreted, etc.).

As you may be able to see from this list, error is a possibility at every stage of the research process and is hazardous to the quality of the data. Therefore it is essential to understand each step well, respect the guidelines for doing good research, and think through the goals and objectives of the entire project before embarking on the actual field work. This applies equally to research where you "just want to ask an expert for an opinion" as well as to a study that may take the form of a full-blown consumer survey. It also applies to archival research, where you are also posing questions of the materials and are subject to sampling and interpretive errors.

We'll look at each of these areas in turn.

Defining Questions   A primary predictor of efficiency and success in the research process is how carefully and how well you formulate the central question or questions that will guide the project. This is particularly important when you are faced with the millions of gigabytes of data that the Internet holds. If a research question is too broad when you march into your local library, you may come away with a couple of dozen books and articles to read and not be too happy about it. On the Internet, an overly broad question may result in a flood of data that takes hours—even days—just to download. Or the reverse may happen in either case; an insufficiently focused question returns no meaningful associated materials. Too often researchers rush into a project with a vague idea of what they're looking for and come away frustrated because they failed to define their question to the point where it would truly be researchable. One good test of a research question is whether you can break it down into smaller, more focused questions. If you can do this rather easily, the chances are good that the question is too broad.

It is also important to thoroughly understand and define all the *terms* you use in your research question or questions. For example, in George Gerbner's well-known annual study of a week of prime-time television, his researchers are examining many aspects of television content, including "the number of acts of violence." The concept of "violence" seems on the surface to be basic and well understood. However, in the task of recognizing and studying violence on television, the researcher must decide whether or not violence includes such behaviors as sarcasm, arguing, and emotional abuse or whether it refers only to physical aggression. Also, what kind of physical agression is violent? Hitting? Shoving? A "playful" slap on the shoulder?

Careful planning will have a positive impact on your ability to estimate the amount of time the study will take and how much it might cost (if you will incur hourly costs or must use fee-based services). Typically, the more focused and defined your research question is, the more efficient your efforts will be.

Sampling Issues   The quality of the sample (who you will talk to or what content you will examine) has everything to do with the overall quality of the final research findings. To illustrate, one of the common motivations for doing research is to be able to generalize from the results of the research to a larger arena (i.e., "all the students on this campus," "all the people in the United States," the "biogenetic literature"). Such generalization is not valid unless a certain type of sampling procedure is used—in this case probability sampling. A **probability sample** is one in which every member of the population has an equal chance of being selected so that the resulting sample is representative of the population from which it was drawn. Without this special and rigorous form of sampling, it is impossible to confidently make generalizations beyond "this is what was true of this sample when I studied them at such and such a time." Moreover, probability sampling allows you to calculate the amount of error associated with different sample sizes, whereas nonprobability sampling does not. In many cases probability sampling and the resulting generalizability are not necessarily desirable, but everyone conducting research should have a clear picture of *why* a particular sampling method and sample were chosen and what he or she gains or gives up by making this choice.

Sampling, as it applies to Internet data and human populations, presents special problems. For example, the difficulty of using the Internet for research is that no one really knows the exact boundaries of either of these resources (people or data), and without this knowledge it is impossible to confidently employ probability sampling techniques. This is true because without being able to describe what is online, or how many people of what types are using the Internet, it is not feasible to draw representative samples. If I sent a survey through a Usenet post (NOT recommended at this time for reasons that will be discussed shortly) hoping for some responses, I might obtain some interesting anecdotal material, but certainly not data that I could present as typical or representative of Internet users. Remember, any sampling procedure that does not give the researcher full control over selection of the respondents is not generalizable. A sample that is selected based on convenience or the self-selection of respondents does not allow the calculation of error, cannot be assumed to be representative, and even violates the assumptions of most statistical procedures (which require probability sampled data to work properly).

Even though it is several years since the commercial world "discovered" the Internet, virtually nothing is known about typical users, let alone specific subgroups, except what can be roughly inferred from overall traffic statistics. The diffuseness of the Internet, the famed intolerance of Internet users for junk solicitations, and even the high rate of growth all combine to make the Internet an improbable site for generalizable survey research.

Methodological Choices   The availability of a reliable sample obviously has an impact on what tools might be best suited for the question or questions at hand. For example, if a probability sample is not obtainable, a survey (requiring analysis with statistical tests requiring larger probability samples) might not be the best choice for the job. Better, more detailed information might be obtained by studying discussion group archives or conducting in-depth interviews over the Internet. The relative quality of Internet archival data sources is also an important consideration. If the online resources for a subject are neither comprehensive nor reliable in the conventional sense, then data analysis and interpretation may be faulty.

Traditionally, research has been categorized as either primary or secondary. Primary research refers to research conducted personally by the researcher or research team. Methods used for primary research include content analysis, discourse analysis, and various types of interviewing (personal, survey, focus group, etc.). Secondary research involves the analysis of data previously gathered by others. Here I use the term *secondary* mainly to describe archival research and analysis of databases, two common activities for Net researchers.

Primary Research

CONTENT ANALYSIS AND DISCOURSE ANALYSIS

The Internet provides perhaps unparalleled opportunities to conduct content and discourse analyses, with its 10,000+ continuous discussion groups on an amazing variety of subjects and thousands of archives of discussions and interactions among users. For content analysts interested in popular press, television shows, or other texts, there are television show transcripts, news reports, online newspapers and articles, and electronic texts by the millions. Because online texts can be searched with all kinds of powerful electronic tools, much of the drudgery is taken out of the coding phase of content analysis. When I recently introduced a friend who was writing a dissertation on the works of Jane Austen to the complete online works of Austen (courtesy of Project Gutenberg, a university-based project to digitize classic books and bring them online), she was overjoyed once she realized that her theories on courtship and romance in Austen's books could now be easily supported by a series of Boolean and proximity searches that would have taken months or perhaps years if done by hand. Likewise, discourse and communication analysts traditionally constrained by laborious transcription of conversations can, if their research includes interests in computer-mediated communication, bypass transcription and focus on the data earlier and more efficiently than before.

Any good text on research methods will include a primer on the conduct of content or discourse analysis; however, keep in mind these two cautions:

1. Sampling Internet resources is problematic due to the shifting and incomplete nature of the network. Be careful about the claims you make about Internet-derived data. Be certain of its source and avoid characterizing results as representative unless you have very good reasons to believe they are. (In the near future it is doubtful whether any research on the Internet can meet strict tests of representativeness and generalizability. Expect to be challenged if you try to present your work as "representing the Internet user," etc.)

2. Internet experts are split over whether or not it is ethical to use the artifacts of human interaction over the Internet as research subjects without first obtaining the explicit consent of all involved. Some feel that if the researcher follows standard ethical practice and assures the confidentiality of all individuals (never revealing the identity of subjects, not matching individual

responses with names, etc.), then the discussions taking place on the Internet become "publicly observable behaviors." Many researchers feel that we all implicitly agree to possible scrutiny when we engage in public behaviors. Others disagree and insist that Usenet and other sites of Internet discussion are private by virtue of their segmented, by-subscription-only nature (even though there are no membership requirements for most lists other than requesting to be added). Researchers must struggle with this ethical question themselves, but in *all cases* researchers must follow accepted ethical standards and practices when conducting research, *particularly when there is the potential for harm* to human subjects.

INTERVIEWS

The Internet links a global network of human resources—experts in many fields, scientists, governments, citizens, consumer markets, journalists, students, educators, and business people. It is a powerful tool for connecting you with others who would not have been accessible otherwise. In the past journalists were notorious for their rows of thick Rolodex files (which they were forced to keep so that at a moment's notice they could find an expert in any area). Now they are using the Internet to place "calls" for experts and authorities in obscure areas. Most journalists have found this method extremely effective, proving to be both quicker and wider in scope in bringing interviewees to them than keeping extensive, quickly outdated paper files. It has surprised many new users that senators and congressmen often respond to questions posed via the Internet, or that Nobel prizewinning scientists answer E-mail from aspiring freshmen chemists. Although the willingness of Internet users to respond to unsolicited requests may decline as network traffic (and overload) increases, for the moment we enjoy a special and privileged relationship to other network users. It is important not to abuse that relationship and to respect both the Internet culture and the privacy of others on the network. Whether your research involves a casual question of another user or an extensive survey design, you must give careful consideration to (1) whether or not it is essential to require the time and effort of another person to answer your key research question(s), (2) whether your research design respects the privacy and culture of those with whom you seek to interact, and (3) what will be the potential impact of your research on others.

Journalists often interview experts over the Internet in one of two ways: (1) in an interactive, real-time chat mode, as with **internet relay chat (IRC),** or in a **multi-user domain (MUD)** or (2) by electronic mail, submitting a list of questions to be answered by the subject and returned at his or her convenience . Either method of conducting a personal interview is considerably cheaper and in many respects easier than trying to connect with someone over the telephone, then paying long-distance tolls to talk. Journalists have reported that they receive more thoughtful, detailed answers to questions posed this way, and as a bonus they do not have to transcribe audiotapes after the interview. They simply download the "transcript" from IRC or the electronic mail exchange and cut and paste directly from it, which of course reduces the chance of misquoting interviewees.

As a substitute for in-person interviewing, this method has both strengths and weaknesses. While online interviewing greatly reduces or eliminates interviewer bias (the subtle cues concerning "how to answer" that interviewees can pick up from an interviewer's tone of voice, dress, or demeanor), a great deal of information may be missed without direct contact with the interviewee. Perhaps most important is the fact that relatively little is known about the influence computers have on communication behaviors and patterns. How does a computer, mediating between two human subjects, alter the form or meaning of a message? Does a computerized interface privilege certain types of personalities or communication styles and not others? These are the kinds of questions for which answers must be obtained before we can adequately evaluate the potential of the Internet for human communication research.

SURVEYS

Despite the recent release of commercial software that allows the collection of survey data through the WWW (SurveySaid for the Web), survey research on the Internet has mostly proved to be unsatisfactory. Currently several different research teams are attempting to profile the Internet usership, and all have been frustrated by a number of problems, the most critical of which is:

> There is *no tolerance* on the Internet for broadcast messages, including unsolicited questionnaires and survey announcements. This practice is called *spamming* and is dealt with very severely, usually resulting in extensive *flaming* by other users and the loss of Internet access privileges at the very least. Researchers are limited to discreet "cross-posts" in selected newsgroups, sites, and a few other locations that reach very little of the overall Net audience. Therefore, survey researchers cannot obtain large or representative samples, which seriously reduces the applicability of their results.

I talk more about spamming in the section on "Ethics and Internet Culture" later in this chapter. For the moment, I conclude that the

Internet is unsuited to survey research, except as a way of collecting anecdotal evidence or experiences and then only under special circumstances. For example, researchers working on a project could develop a WWW homepage or Gopher site detailing the purpose of the project, perhaps even containing the downloadable questionnaire itself. The researchers could announce and describe the project in the major search engines and directories (such as Yahoo, Lycos, Mosaic) and invite participants. In this way, the researchers avoid spamming and provide a way to attract interested parties to the project without distributing the questionnaire to anyone who might be offended or annoyed by it. In general, students should tread cautiously before using any kind of large-scale survey effort because a misstep can have serious consequences.

ELECTRONIC FOCUS GROUPS

Despite the problems of doing survey research within its environment, the Internet does currently provide a cost-effective means of reaching specific demographic groups for exploratory or qualitative research. For example, a large multimedia title publisher regularly recruits participants for paid focus groups from several Usenet groups. These respondents are brought together for in-depth discussions to evaluate concepts, potential advertising, packaging, and other elements. Some respondents are asked to beta-test new products. Focus groups are also used to probe into the emotive level of the relationship between products and purchase behavior. Some companies are experimenting with conducting such focus groups online. Because focus groups are quite expensive when done in the traditional manner (renting a special facility and paying the travel costs of a skilled moderator plus fees for the respondents, etc. can cost from $5,000 to $10,000 per group or more), using the Internet to conduct these group discussions offers tremendous opportunities to cut costs and at the same time reach specialized audiences. The addition of videoconferencing as a routine computing function will make this kind of research even more attractive and efficient. However, focus groups or individually conducted in-depth interviews cannot be used for more than directional information and are therefore limited in their application.

Archival Research Issues

Archival research means digging into existing databases and texts, searching for specific data or topics. While most library catalogs feature standardized search engines, the Internet's nascent search facilities differ widely in their capabilities and potential. Doing meaningful archival or secondary research on the Internet requires the patience to try triangulated searches with multiple search engines and directories, and even more fortitude to sort through what could be hundreds or thousands of "hits" (search results returned to you listing what the search engines "think" are matches).

Interestingly, some experts believe that the rush by libraries to scrap their card catalogs in favor of more accessible online catalogs considerably weakens the researchers' ability to collocate or cross-reference material.[2] According to critics, online catalogers inputting old paper cards are not versed in the long-standing Library of Congress "Rules of Interpretation" and omit multiple subject headings and notes because database design is usually too rigid to accept the kind of free-form text allowed by card catalogs. The hypertext capability of the WWW helps overcome this problem by allowing the researcher to follow "links" or associated concepts/sources easily, tunneling further into related data much as a good reference librarian would do when noting "*see* xxxx and *see also* yyyy" on a paper card.

Keyword searches, Boolean searches, proximity searches, and other techniques are compensation for the loss of card catalog collocations, but these bring with them the need to think carefully because inappropriate search terms can waste precious time. Defining terms and research questions before approaching data collection is as essential in archival research as in the other methods; keyword choices are intimately related to the important definitions and concepts that researchers delineate in the planning stage.

A full discussion of search engines relevant to each Internet service is given in Part 3.

The Ethics of Data Collection

Any research project arguably has the potential to create change, and the consequences of that change must be carefully considered by the researchers. Researchers must ask themselves at least two critical questions before beginning any study:

1. Who or what might be *hurt* by this research?

2. Who or what might be *helped* by this research?

While it is not always possible to foresee all the potential impact of a particular research question or research design, researchers generally err on the side of caution, particularly when the subjects of their research are other human beings. At the very least, most researchers agree that by studying something we change it, no matter how much we might try not to do so. However, we can attempt to minimize our impact. Accepted research practice includes ensuring that human subjects must be respected and protected by the researcher. That protection includes:

- *Informed consent procedures.* Informed consent means that researchers tell the people who will be part of the study what the purpose of the project is, what their involvement includes, and what is the intended use of the results. Many projects benefit from a further debriefing after the project is complete so that subjects can ask questions and learn the research results if they wish.

- *Confidentiality.* Researchers must be prepared to promise, and deliver, confidentiality. This means that the identity of individual subjects is *never* connected with their answers to your questions. This can sometimes take considerable proactive effort; for example, if your sample is small and consists of "heads of major U.S. motion picture studios," it would not take much personal description for someone familiar with that industry to associate an individual's responses to his or her commentary, as in "Subject X, a 36-year-old blonde and the youngest female executive ever to control a major studio, reported that ageism is rampant in Hollywood." Disguising identities and still providing enough descriptive information about the sample to give the data context can be tricky. However, because you cannot predict the repercussions of loss of subject confidentiality, you must make extraordinary efforts to preserve it. Be aware that confidentiality is different from anonymity, which is available only when researchers themselves cannot identify the subjects. Because researchers usually require some identifying information for interview verification or follow-up, anonymity can never really be delivered. Finally, confidentiality includes never giving or selling your sample or subject list to others without the express consent of your subjects.

Ethical research procedures also require that researchers avoid the temptation of misrepresenting their data by "fudging" or dishonest manipulation, whether the data are a document, responses from a survey, or commentary from individuals.

Ethics and the Internet Culture

Serious questions arise about how research through the Internet complies with the basic accepted criteria for ethical conduct of research.

How does a researcher, for example, ensure that confidentiality for all subjects will be rigorously maintained, when all forms of electronic mail on the Internet are not guaranteed to be secure? When all Net traffic leaves a **digital vapor trail**, how can a researcher provide assurances that a respondent's identity will never be "matched" with his or her responses? Informed consent procedures must be reconceptualized to cope with the complexity of the Internet. In the interim, researchers should be honest about what they can and cannot reasonably deliver in terms of confidentiality and security.

Furthermore, the Internet has its own codes of conduct and ethical standards that researchers seeking to work within the Internet environment must respect. The Internet is really a community, although a global and virtual one. What is particularly interesting about the evolution of the Internet is that essentially it has no central organization. It is a kind of new society formed entirely by the consensus of users. *Newsweek* recently referred to the Internet as "the Wild West. No one owns it . . . it has no rules." However, it *does* have rules, a set of ethical standards designed to protect and advise users. These guidelines are essential for the smooth functioning of the entire network.

The very nature of electronic communication raises new moral issues. Issues that need to be addressed include privacy of mail, personal identities, access and control of the network, pornographic or unwanted messages, copyright, and commercial uses of the network. Most businesses and institutions with Internet access have agreed to an **acceptable use policy (AUP)** and have developed their own AUPs that govern access from their sites. An AUP is the way an organization informs users of its expectations and responsibilities. Earlier in this book, I advised you to ask for the AUP statements from your university computing center or from the organization that supplies your Internet access. This is important because you are expected to follow these policies *without exception*.

One of the major concerns of organizations connected to the Internet is that some users selfishly or intentionally disrupt network traffic, crashing the network and its connected systems. The potential for various types of crime (fraudulent use of computing resources; theft of data, equipment, or intellectual property; unauthorized access; forgery; etc.) is great and means that organizations must protect themselves and limit their liabilities. If a system administrator finds that you have been guilty of actions—whether inconsiderate or malicious—that are a threat to other users or to the network itself, you will probably find your account privileges rescinded or severely restricted.

The best rule of thumb is to try to anticipate the results of your actions when you are using Internet resources and to refrain from behaviors that could cause problems. *Consideration for others* should be a watchword, and if you do not practice it, others will do it for you, either by removing you from the Net or making it very uncomfortable for you to be there. **Flames** are one way Internet users police themselves; people who do not behave like good citizens (or "netizens") are sent reproving and sometimes blistering messages. These are embarrassing, at a minimum. In some cases, flaming reached such intensity that network traffic slowed noticeably due to the high volume of mail exchange, sometimes forcing a system administrator to temporarily remove a server from the network. If you incite a flame war and your sysadmin experiences traffic problems because of it, you can be certain there will be more repercussions for you than an overstuffed E-mail box. For the Internet to continue to function smoothly, everyone on it must respect the other's reasons for being there, and although it is easy to forget in the midst of a fascinating MUD exchange that the Net is a place for *real work*, we must all make sure that it continues to be a productive environment for work. As the Internet Activities Board says: "The Internet exists in the general research milieu. Portions of it continue to be used to support research and experimentation on networking. Because experimentation on the Internet has the potential to affect all of its components and users, researchers have the responsibility to exercise extreme caution in the conduct of their work. Negligence in the conduct of Internet-wide experiments is both irresponsible and unacceptable."

A great deal has been written about Internet culture, particularly in 1994 when **newbies** (novice users) from homes and businesses flooded onto the Internet in great numbers. Previously, the Internet was a tightly knit and fairly homogeneous community consisting mostly of government and university scientists and researchers. Many of these long-time Internet users were instrumental in building the network itself over the past ten years, setting policies, and adding servers and resources. As with many small communities, many of the "rules of the road" were unwritten but well understood by the initiated. The millions of new users without a vested interest in the creation of the Internet who recently jumped in with both feet have created a kind of culture clash, because many of the policies that contributed to the smooth functioning of the Internet were not made explicit to these new users until they unwittingly trespassed upon them. In self-defense, the old-timers have sometimes reacted very strongly to these transgressions, particularly in cases of **spamming** (unsolicited messages sent to many unrelated groups or individuals). Any new user who expects to work and play on the Internet should take the time to become thoroughly familiar with the various expectations of Internet culture and respect these in all dealings.

Spamming

It's possible, even easy, to get a list of all the 10,000+ Usenet newsgroups as well as the thousands of publicly accessible Listserv lists. With a little technical expertise and the help of a basic handbook on programming, you can write a code that will mail a single message to every one of these groups. This fact has not escaped unscrupulous marketers who do not understand the nature of the Internet, nor has it escaped those with obsessive opinions they want to air. However, the resulting global **flame wars** and ostracisms of the offenders were truly awe-inspiring. The consequences of such inconsiderate and disruptive behavior are not easily forgotten. Spammers are the targets of a global flame war, which results in many nasty messages directed at the spammer and his or her system administrator (who will promptly close the spammer's account and bar that person from the system). Spammers may also be the target of a **mailbombing**, where others send so much flame mail to the spammer that it causes their system to crash. In the spring of 1995, a class action suit was formed by several Internet users against parties they thought had sent them junk E-mail. The lawsuit is the first to seek an extension of the rights now enjoyed by owners of fax machines, so there may soon be legal retribution for spamming. In addition, the bad reputation of spammers lingers on the Internet for a long time.

Since early 1994, there have been at least three such mailings that managed to reach thousands of discussion groups and individuals all over the world. One of the offenders warned of the end of the world, one sent a kind of chain letter labeled MAKE.MONEY.FAST (like the tattered flyers one sees around Laundromats and grocery stores), but the most-publicized one was the Canter & Siegel message concerning their "Green Card Lottery." Canter and Siegel, a pair of immigration attorneys, later published a book in which they claimed that the Internet was simply "an ideal, low-cost and perfectly legitimate way to target people likely to be potential clients."

Many Internet users disagreed with them for various reasons. First, many of the charters of the Usenet newsgroups and Listservs specifically prohibit business solicitations. One of the main complaints about the rapid commercialization of the Internet over the past year is that businesses enter the network with communication models more suited to a broadcast environment such as television or radio, where time and space have direct economic costs, information must be compressed, image is more important than solid data, and massive audiences must be simultaneously addressed with a single message in order to be cost effective. On the contrary, the Internet as a business environment opens the possibility of establishing personalized customer relationships and custom message systems, which advertising research has shown to be very effective in moving people through the sales cycle and stimulating positive product and brand image associations. Therefore, the spamming lawyers were ignorantly applying old technology to an entirely new business frontier, and to no avail. The pair, far from "making a fortune on the Information Superhighway" as their book claims, probably made less than $100,000 from the entire caper, which is hardly a fortune and no doubt much less than they could have grossed by following responsible and targeted Internet marketing practices!

Another objection to spamming is that although the Internet seems to be free of cost (other than the cost of a connection or a local call to the server), it certainly is not. One popular newsreader, "tin," displays the following message before it passes your message through the system:

> This program posts news articles to thousands of machines throughout the entire civilized world. Your message will cost the Net hundreds if not thousands of dollars to send everywhere. Please be sure you know what you are doing.

Servers all over the world must exchange packets, tie up expensive high-capacity telephone lines, and take time from other tasks to move messages around. Sending junk E-mail may not appear to have a direct cost attached to it, but someone, somewhere, is paying. This is why spamming is undoubtedly one of the most despised of all illicit Internet activities and is dealt with so severely.

Finally, people who gather to discuss a topic get annoyed when someone discusses something outside the group's charter, referred to as "off-topic posts." They often complain to the newsgroup itself, thereby increasing the traffic even further and wasting the time of everyone following that group's discussion. Read the groups **FAQ (frequently asked questions)** file before posting anything to a group, and also monitor the discussion for a while before you participate to make sure that what you want to say is within the accepted boundaries of their subject area.

THE CANCELMOOSE AND CANCELBOTS

As a way to discourage and ultimately prevent spamming over the Internet, some enterprising but unidentified hacker wrote a program known as **Cancelmoose**, which monitors worldwide Usenet posts and automatically cancels messages if the software (and/or the Cancelmoose author) detects that a single message is being sent to multiple groups. The number of messages or the threshold above which all messages to groups get canceled is not known, but what is certain is that researchers cannot use "broadcast messaging" through Usenet or

Listservs to solicit survey participants, ask for pointers to data or experts, or ask other questions simultaneously of multiple groups.

The Cancelmoose is now a fact of Internet life and no doubt the forerunner of other spam-preventative measures, but it is not without controversy. Although some Internet users believe that Cancelmoose provides a much-needed public service, others feel that it is an infringement of Freedom of Speech rights and could be used to silence points of view at odds with the Cancelmoose. In fact, cruder **cancelbot** programs are popping up on interactive discussion forums as an addition to flame wars, where your opponent simply cancels your messages whenever you appear there and thus prevents your interaction with others on the site. Obviously, this trend has the potential to affect the conduct of research and business on the Net if an adversary can easily make your presence invisible or otherwise interfere with your work by using cancelbots or other smart agents.

The best rule of thumb to follow is to post *only* when you are convinced (and have exercised due diligence to ensure) that you are posting *on-topic* for that discussion group, meaning that the subject is within the group's charter and relevant to current interests. Secondly, never post messages simultaneously to multiple groups.

The Computer Ethics Institute in Washington, D.C., has developed "Ten Commandments of Computing," which the Internet Activities Board and other major entities endorse:

THE TEN COMMANDMENTS FOR COMPUTER ETHICS
from the Computer Ethics Institute

1. Thou shalt not use a computer to harm other people.

2. Thou shalt not interfere with other people's computer work.

3. Thou shalt not snoop around in other people's files.

4. Thou shalt not use a computer to steal.

5. Thou shalt not use a computer to bear false witness.

6. Thou shalt not use or copy software for which you have not paid.

7. Thou shalt not use other people's computer resources without authorization.

8. Thou shalt not appropriate other people's intellectual output.

9. Thou shalt think about the social consequences of the program you write.

10. Thou shalt use a computer in ways that show consideration and respect.

Play it safe and take the time to think through what you need to find out. Balance it against consideration of others.

Subject your research goals to these additional tests:[3]

1. *Informed consent.* When in doubt about performing any particular action, inform those whom your action will affect of your intentions and obtain their consent when applicable.

2. *The higher ethic.* Take the action that achieves the greater good.

3. *Most restrictive action.* Take the action, or avoid the action, by assuming the most severe consequences that could happen.

4. *Kantian universality rule.* If an act or failure to act is not right for everyone to commit, then it is not right for anyone to commit.

5. *Descartes' change rule.* A sufficient change in degree produces a change in kind. Whereas many small losses may be acceptable individually, taken as a whole, they may result in unacceptable losses.

6. *Owners' conservative rule.* Assume that others will treat your assets as belonging in the public domain. Explicitly declare the products of your efforts and your property to be either private or public in reasonably visible ways.

7. *Users' conservative rule.* Assume that any tangible or intangible item belongs to somebody else unless an explicit declaration or convention identifies it as being in the public domain or authorized for your use.

Research Collaboration

The expansion of new information technologies, of which the Internet is an unparalleled example, offers unique opportunities for "individuals and organizations to focus on collaboration."[4] Research efforts are often collaborative because it is more powerful to bring together individuals with different strengths and skills to work on a single project than to have one person do it. In the past collaboration has been a complicated affair because appropriate research partners are not always favored with close physical proximity to each other or to the resources they need. The Internet makes possible the development of a temporary and flexible "virtual organization" that is linked by technology to share skills, costs, and access to resources. In fact, when universities began to use the Internet in the mid-1980s, one of the primary uses was to link researchers at different institutions so that they could easily share data and computing resources. The occasion of my first brush with the Internet was my need to send a large datafile to a colleague at another university with whom I was collaborating on an article. Splitting the file onto 25+ floppy disks and mailing it across the country looked expensive and time consuming. Instead, I learned about **file transfer protocol (FTP)** and sent it over the Internet in a few seconds. After that, I was hooked. Later, we sent drafts of our article back and forth through E-mail, editing each other's work and finally ending with a polished piece. Today, I do the same thing with book publishers, journal editors, and clients. I have found that the Internet is a way to vastly increase the efficiency of collaborative efforts and maximize my access to people and resources. It will become even more powerful as additional interactive and "groupware" applications are added that allow "whiteboard" conferencing at the same time as reliable audio and videoconferencing.[5]

Some experts believe that as businesses and the workplace move online, hierarchies and organizations will flatten out until, ultimately, workers will be brought together in a temporary "virtual space" on a project-by-project basis. This situation will realize tremendous cost savings for businesses (eliminating the need for office buildings, new highways to drive to them, and permanent payrolls), and it will allow many more businesses to benefit from the synergy of a constantly shifting, highly experienced workforce. Michael Schrage is interested in the future of collaboration in the workplace and various creative fields. He believes that collaborative tools such as the Internet "will create a fundamental paradigm shift and alter our sense of community. For Schrage, collaboration—both conceptual and technical—is a necessary way of coping with the increasing complexity of everyday life in an era of specialization."[6]

Online collaboration is likely to be a fact of working life in the future, but it can also contribute to productivity now. Seek opportunities to collaborate with others in your field whenever possible.

Data Analysis: A Creative Process

The hardest fact to grasp about the Internet and the I-way is this: It isn't a thing; it isn't an entity; it isn't an organization. No one owns it; no one runs it. It is simply Everyone's Computers, Connected.

James Gleick, Founder of *The Pipeline,* NYC, 1994

EVALUATING THE QUALITY OF DATA

When I first saw it, James Gleick's observation struck me as one of the best definitions of the Internet and what it is really about. Its autonomy and spontaneity are often described as approaching the Jeffersonian ideal of democracy. However, it is also an excellent statement of one of the Internet's primary weaknesses—that there is no central authority and therefore no quality control. This lack of quality control is one of the greatest problems researchers face when considering the Internet as a source for data because it places a greater burden of responsibility on researchers to evaluate the quality and integrity of *every single source*. In a library full of books and journals, the relative credibility of sources appears simple to ascertain. Some publishers and authors are considered more prestigious than others, but most printed matter that has passed through an editorial or review process is considered to be at least reliable if not accurate. Unfortunately, a relatively small percentage of Internet data are derived from mainstream publications or publishing houses. Quite a lot of it reflects the idiosyncratic opinion, practice, or ideas of an individual or organization who simply wanted to share. Conversely, the Internet is often described as a "content intensive environment," where the depth and detail of information are valued over glitz and its resulting reductionism. Some of the material will surprise you in its richness and scope of supporting evidence. Still, if the Internet data I am considering is not direct from a credible government source (such as the U.S. Census Bureau or the SEC), I take the time to apply evaluative criteria to it by asking the following questions:

1. Can I independently verify information offered as fact? (Is the origin of the data mentioned? Are other source materials or references listed? Are there sources I trust against which I can check one or more of the assertions, statistics, or facts?)

2. How was this information obtained? (Is the author a noted expert? Is the information the result of a custom study that followed accepted research practice? Is it a compilation of secondary research? Is it editorial opinion? Does the author provide convincing support for his or her assertions? What are the author's affiliations? Is he or she speaking on behalf of an employer or as a private citizen? And so on.)

3. Do the conclusions offered follow logically from the evidence offered in the argument?

As you can see, the first step in evaluating the quality of a source lies in testing the logic of and evidence for the offered argument. If information is simply opinion, then it need not be subjected to many rigorous tests if you contextualize it as opinion in your work. However, if data are presented as *facts*, they must be checked for accuracy, using as many credible sources as possible as a cross-check. Avoid compounding research errors by passing on data from sources that are not credible.

For example, suppose you were asked to write an article for the campus newspaper on the impact of NAFTA in the area in which you live. This is a typical assignment, but your deadline is just four hours away! You think you can go online to gather background material for your story. You are looking for at least these three types of information:

1. Opinions of local residents concerning NAFTA's effects on them.

2. Experts who have followed NAFTA closely and are willing to be quoted.

3. Official backgrounders, statistics, and economic information about NAFTA and its effects.

Here's what I'd do to find this data:

- Finding local resident opinions online is relatively straightforward. I would go into Usenet and look for local Usenet discussion groups or even statewide or regional discussion groups. For example, in my home town of San Diego, there are several Usenet groups: sd.chat, sd.politics, sd.misc, as well as many California-wide groups—i.e., ca.politics. Any of these might be a good spot for a polite post asking for opinions on my topic. Alternatively, with the short deadline I might just scan through the recent posts looking for discussions or "threads" related to my topic and then contact individuals by electronic mail for speedy feedback. Of course, with local subjects I can always pick up the phone!

- For experts on NAFTA, I could do a number of things. First, I'd probably take a look at the online "Who's Who on the Internet" just on the chance that a NAFTA specialist or international economist might be listed. Next, I would look at the Usenet list or the Listserv list (private discussion groups conducted by E-mail) for specific discussions related to NAFTA or Latin American–North American trade. Ha! I've found a university-based moderated Listserv group on NAFTA. I take a look at the group's FAQ (Frequently Asked Questions) file posted on the WWW and learn where the group's archives are kept. Reading these, I find several frequent contributors to the discussion with impressive credentials and interesting opinions. I send E-mail to all of these with a request for quick feedback to my questions (again, because phone numbers are often attached to E-mail messages in the "signature" lines, I might pick up the phone at this point and try to reach my list of experts that way. Another way to find out who might be active in a field and interested in discussing the topic with others is to send the Listserv a message to "review" the group. The "review" command will send statistics on list activity by contributor, which is very useful if the group's archives are not available (more on the specifics of Listservs in the next section).

- The final document search is a bit trickier. As a first step, I would request a file search using a powerful WWW search engine like Lycos or Webcrawler, probably with the single keyword "NAFTA." This type of search will return many documents. Quite a few are within the FED-WORLD system (the U.S. government's unified server interface for many of its federal agencies' databases), and in fact the entire Congressional Record related to the passage and tracking of NAFTA is available there. This is a good source because government data are generally reliable. However, several dozen nongovernment and non-U.S. documents are also identified. How do I go about examining these? A reporter will look at all of the issues just discussed: paying attention to the credibility of the source, if known; independently verifying the facts and figures mentioned in the documents; and spending some time to get a feel for the validity of the data and the opinions expressed in documents from sources not personally known to the researcher or without the aura of credibility that government and university-generated data seem to command. As a further check on validity before using any data from these documents, I would take the opportunity to run key points by my panel of "experts" for their reaction and feedback.

On almost any issue that might become a topic for research, there will be several viewpoints. A responsible researcher makes sure that as far as possible all reasonable perspectives are represented so that a balanced assessment can be achieved. Do not be too eager to accept "consensus" between people or data sources because it is almost certainly not the entire story.

Ultimately, if I have taken care to be reasonably sure that the information I am using is reliable and accurate, the Internet is probably the *most efficient* way to produce thoroughly researched articles and reports. I have even heard journalists remark that in an era of accelerating deadlines, it is possibly the only way to quickly assemble such a large variety of widely dispersed perspectives and data sources.

EXAMINING PATTERNS

Once data is collected, research almost always involves exploring that data for meaningful patterns, working to make sense of it. There are all kinds of systematic techniques for data analysis, such as content coding, ethnographic description, contextual coding, and statistics, to name just a few. However, it is essential that researchers remember that *patterns are what matter, not idiosyncratic incidents or observations*. In other words, while it is tempting to pick out some particularly juicy tidbit from a dataset and use it as representative of the whole, this is misleading unless it truly represents a common pattern within the dataset. Select an appropriate method of data analysis and be rigorous in your application of it until your findings emerge. Then, and only then, be "creative" in your interpretation and speculations; avoid using isolated data to prove a private point as this is neither a valid nor an ethical use of research data.

STATISTICS

Some research methods require the expression of data in numerical terms, such as survey research and content analysis. Quantitative data are usually best analyzed by statistical tests, some of which assume that probability sampling has been used (this is true of inferential or multivariate statistics). Because of the sampling problems associated with the Internet, however, statistical tests that assume the property of a random sample should be avoided or used with extreme caution. Any good research primer will provide further direction on the use of statistics and the assumptions of individual tests.

Fair Use, Copyright, and Attribution

So far I have emphasized the "free availability" and abundance of materials on the Internet. Resources are freely available; it is almost too easy (compared to going to a library) to push a button and download an article, database, or message to your hard drive where you can edit it, read it, print it, or merge it with other information. However, it is easy to overlook the fact that information is intellectual property, whether delivered electronically, in print, or in person, and simply downloading something does not make it yours. Rather, copyright laws apply to Internet data and print materials equally. Although there are currently some lively debates centering around fair use and copyright as they pertain to a chaotic international (and unregulated) network like the Internet, most legal opinions firmly support the rights of individuals, businesses, publishers, and others who assert that they own the rights to their own data. Soon the network will need to deal with how to track ethically access to materials so that authors can be paid royalties for their work. This controversy is already heating up.

For researchers there is an added concern with correct attribution. All sources of information must be cited so that others can evaluate the premises and evidence in the work for themselves. Attribution styles for electronic sources are also quite different from those used for print materials. An excellent and comprehensive guide to how to cite materials from online or electronic sources is Xia Li and Nancy Crane's book *Electronic Style: A Guide to Citing Electronic Information* (Meckler, 1993). However, some rules of thumb are:

1. When citing from a book or magazine article, it is accepted practice to tell readers how to find the book or article for themselves by referencing the publisher, journal, or book title, year of publication, and page numbers. This in effect is the *location* of the source. On the Internet, information you decide to use is also drawn from a specific location, usually expressed as a *path* statement or address as in:

   http://www.harris.com/book.html

   Using this path statement, readers can see that if they want to find that same source material they should look on the WWW at the address *www.harris.com* and that the file name containing the data is *book.html*. It is important to record path information exactly, avoiding typographic errors of any kind (computers are very literal that way and will reject a path if so much as a period or space is misplaced or missing).

   Note: If a path statement uses all lowercase, all uppercase, or a mixture of upper and lowercase letters, be certain to replicate it exactly because the UNIX programming language in use at most Internet servers today is case sensitive.

2. Full information should be provided as to the date you accessed the material, primarily because "publications" on the Internet can potentially go "out of print" much sooner than printed material. Information is moved from a server or withdrawn, or a server may change addresses or names, or the path structure may simply change a bit and suddenly readers will find that they cannot verify your information. If the date is provided (some researchers even include the time of day), readers can at least see at what point the path statement was correct, which might be of help if someone really wanted to track down a resource.

3. To cite a source from an online database, use the following format:

   Database title. [Online path statement]. (year, month, day). Available: Publisher Name. File: subdirectory of file name where data was found.

A WWW example is:

SRI Interactive VALS Server. [http://sri.future.com/vals/valshome.html]. (1995, May). Available: Stanford Research Institute. File: valshome.html.

4. Personal E-mail messages cited in reports or articles should be cited only with permission of the sender. It is also accepted practice to make the message available to others via a publicly accessible location, such as an FTP dropbox or an automated mail responder, and to reference the path of these files after Available E-mail. An accepted format is:

Author. (year, month). *Title* (edition), [Type of medium]. Available E-mail: Message location or command to retrieve file.

An example is:

Kaplan, F. (1994, December). Netiquette Guide. Available E-mail: COMSERVE@RPIECS Message: Get NETIQUETTE GUIDE.

5. To cite files available via FTP (this includes online software, books, and other documents retrieved via FTP), use the following format:

Author. (date). Title (edition), [medium]. Available FTP: path statement and file name.

An example is:

Austen, J. (1994). *Pride and Prejudice* [online]. Available FTP: ftp.austen.edu Directory: pub File: pride.zip

6. To cite files available via Telnet, use the following format:

Author. (date). Title (edition), [medium]. Available Telnet: path statement and file name.

An example is:

Austen, J. (1994). *Pride and Prejudice* [online]. Available Telnet: austen.edu Directory: pub File: pride.zip

7. To cite from a Usenet or Listserv discussion group, obtain the consent of the subjects wherever possible. (Some people use "anonymous reposters" when they participate in discussion groups, which strips out identifying information about the sender and makes them nearly impossible to trace, so obtaining consent may not be possible in all cases.) Use the following format:

Author of message. (year, month day). Topic of discussion or thread [Discussion]. *Group Name* [Online]. Available E-mail: address or command to retrieve file.

A Listserv example is:

Harris, C. (1995, February 5). Internet Research Potential [Discussion]. *Internet Marketing Discussion List* [Online]. Available E-mail: Listserv@market.com

A Usenet example is:

Harris, C. (1995, February 5). Internet Research Potential [Discussion]. *Internet Marketing Discussion List* [Online]. Available E-mail: Usenet Newsgroup: biz.market.news

8. A "forwarded message" is one that was not addressed to you by the original sender but was copied and forwarded to you by the receiver. Again, if I were going to use a forwarded message in my research, I would attempt to contact the original author and ask permission to do so. To cite a forwarded E-mail message, use the following format:

Name of person forwarding the message. (year, month day). Subject of message. Original sender of message, *Forwarded subject of message* [Online]. Available E-mail: address or command to retrieve file.

An example is:

Mitnick, K. (1995, April 1). Justice and Law. Original sender M. Jackson, *Opinions and Ideas* [Online]. Available E-mail: Listserv@law.net

9. If citing only part of a work, include page numbers, line numbers, or record number.

Research Success Stories

By now I have discussed several ways in which the Internet can be used successfully for productive, thorough, and efficient research. In business and education there are thousands of examples of occasions when instant access to the information that the Internet offers "saved the day." In fact, an online network in Waltham, Massachusetts, known as FARNET, began collecting these success stories a couple of years ago and now has a collection that represents Internet users from every state in the United States and some foreign countries. Examples of FARNET stories I find inspirational include:

- As part of a National Science Foundation (NSF) sponsored "Teaching Teleapprenticeships" research project at the University of Illinois, students used the Internet to conduct research in biology and mathematics in an experimental, self-paced course format. Students chose a biology or mathematics challenge from a list of topics that were obtained from several electronic sources such as TheNews. They then used electronic mail to research the topic and communicate with the originator of the challenge or question, who could be anywhere around the world. The students maintained a journal of activities along with personal thoughts about their experiences. They shared those writings on a regular basis with the instructor via the network. They also shared lesson plans, teaching ideas, problems they were having in their classrooms, as well as notes on presentations they attended at a professional mathematics meeting.

- In 1992 Simmons College received funding from the NSF to initiate a "network to improve environmental science education in New England." This project resulted in Environet, in which students can engage in an extensive collaborative environmental monitoring project. Environet teachers and their students, as well as other teachers, have participated in two projects thus far—Acid Rain and Road Kill. Data on the pH of precipitation and types of roadkills have been sent via E-Mail to a bulletin board where the results are posted and thus made available to everyone involved. Mr. Bartlett's students have been particularly involved in organizing, analyzing, and presenting the data from these two projects. By monitoring projects, students are contributing data to a real scientific research project; it will help them understand the value and importance of scientific collaboration. New Hampshire Fish and Game and Massachusetts Division of Fisheries and Wildlife have both expressed interest in the results of the Road Kill project. Another bulletin board is an electronic newsletter edited by three Environet teachers. Information for the newsletter is contributed by the teachers and staff of Environet. The final bulletin board focuses on responses to an "Environmental Question of the Week," posted by the project co-director, to which teachers and students respond. Previous questions have involved the controversy between conservation and development, the most important environmental problems facing the Clinton administration, and the question of whether wolves should be reintroduced into Yellowstone National Park. This bulletin board reinforces the importance of scientific communication and helps students to formulate carefully reasoned arguments on controversial questions that require scientific data to support their decisions.

In this next story, a Canadian doctor based in Malaysia uses the Internet to access the Human Genome Database for patient research. Patricia Haley in Maryland talks about how medical professionals worldwide use her Internet databases for their work.

- "I support users located all over the world for two related databases: Genome Data Base, containing human gene mapping data, and OMIM, a catalog of human genes and genetic disorders. We have had users register from far-flung places such as Russia and Saudi Arabia, but the most amazing interaction with a user I've had so far is the Internet relationship I've developed with a doctor practicing in Malaysia. One morning in June 1992 I came into work and checked my E-mail queue, which receives messages sent to our help alias. One of the messages sent to the help alias, but addressed to me in particular, was from a Dr. Elizabeth Hillman, describing herself as 'a Canadian paediatrician working in an isolated medical school on the underserved East Coast of Malaysia. . . . We have just successfully connected to Internet and have no trouble communicating from here.' I sent her back an E-mail telling her we'd be happy to register her and that I was unaware that I was famous in Malaysia! My co-worker Kerryn Brandt joked with me about a bunch of natives bowing before a Sun workstation chanting, 'Patty Haley, Patty Haley.' Word spread around the office and more than once the comment was heard, 'How isolated can they be if they're on the Internet?' We mailed her a letter containing her **login** and password and shipped her our documentation via UPS. About three weeks later she E-mailed us again to let us know that she had received her letter but was still waiting on the documentation: 'I expect I should wait for my package, but all my colleagues are so keen to get using the database that I am being pressured into contacting you as I am already able to communicate through MIMOS in Kuala Lumpur through Internet.' She then asked us to help her solve a medical mystery of a woman and her premature baby. She described the baby's condition in detail and asked us to find out both if the baby's condition had a name and whether or not the mother's future children could be afflicted. We are normally too short-staffed to perform searches for users, but we decided she was an exception. Kerryn searched on the keywords of the baby's condition in OMIM and forwarded three entries that were relevant. Dr. Hillman and associates were able to diagnose the baby as having Baller-Gerold Syndrome. 'Do you know what something like this means in a really isolated place like this where such information is impossible to find? . . . Maybe you and Kerryn better come to Malaysia for a visit. It is a beautiful country, and our beach is called The Beach of Passionate Love!' She mentioned wishing she could send us orchids by E-mail, but her grateful E-mail was the equivalent. I heard from Dr. Hillman a few times over the summer, and I learned that she got our documentation, but I also learned she was coming back to Canada for her daughter's wedding. Around Christmas, she E-mailed again with greetings and another OMIM question. Dr. Hillman and colleagues are not directly online with their Internet host, which is why they have not begun searching the database themselves, but it is always nice to hear from her. She mentioned in her Christmas query (and greetings) that she would be in Baltimore in May, so we may have an opportunity to meet face-to-face. I hope that we can meet because she represents what user support is all about—people helping people. We couldn't have done it without the Internet!

- On the contributions of Internet-based Creative Writing Groups and Peer Review of Articles, Jerry Seltzer of DEC wrote that "A Notes File at Digital (PROSE) and a newsgroup on the Internet (alt.prose) are both devoted to creative writing—serving as the electronic equivalent of self-help writers' groups. Participants post their own stories and comment on those of others. They freely and openly give their time and effort to help one another improve their writing and find markets. Because this isn't a face-to-face encounter, and because most of the participants do not know one another personally, the criticism tends to be painfully honest, which is what most writers need and crave. The words are judged on their own merit. Sometimes participants who live close to one another arrange for face-to-face social get-togethers. Then when they move back to the electronic realm, their messages take on a more personal tone. But when it comes to critical judgement, the network still seems to foster impartial candor. Many of the joys of the Internet come from the fact that everything doesn't have to be structured and organized. You don't have to ask and wait for permission from some authority. In many cases, you can simply exercise your imagination and initiative, within the bounds of good sense and good taste."

- Stephen P. Berczuk, from MIT, speaks of the collaborative potential of the Internet and his experience working with other scientists over the Internet: "I am currently involved in a NASA sponsored project to develop an X-Ray Astronomy satellite (XTE—the X-Ray Timing Explorer). The software for the project is being developed by 3 groups: *) MIT, Cambridge, MA *) NASA Goddard Space Flight Center, Greenbelt, MD *) UCSD, San Diego, CA. Since the work is distributed among these three sites, communication is essential. We use the Internet to supplement other means of contact such as teleconferences and face-to-face meetings. The uses of the Internet include: *) Exchange of technical documents in text or postscript form *) Exchange of source code *) Detailed technical discussions, which would be difficult to accomplish via phone calls because of scheduling conflicts or the level of technical detail. While the Internet does not remove the need for face-to-face meetings and travel, it reduces the number of them and allows them to be more productive. This may not be the most creative use of the Internet, [but] this project would be nearly impossible to do were it not for the facilities provided by the Internet."

In the next story, University of Utah students use the Internet to explore Italian society and culture from afar.

- "Topics in Italian Culture: Contemporary Issues" was a fourth-year course taught at the University of Utah, spring quarter of 1992, by Maurizio Oliva, moliva@c.utah.edu. It was the last in a series of three courses about the contemporary history, literature, and society of Italy. Six students enrolled, all of whom had achieved advanced levels of proficiency in reading, writing, and speaking Italian. The goals of the course were to increase students' knowledge of Italian society and to engage them in producing authentic text for the purpose of communicating with native speakers about important issues. All aspects of the course were taught in Italian. Students spent the first two weeks reading background material related to Italian society and culture, gathering the basic tools necessary to use the network and choosing the topic that would be the focus of their study during the quarter. The teacher supplied a list of possible topics related to contemporary Italian society, about which students could communicate with native speakers via written text sent on NEWS in the newsgroup called soc.culture.italian. Those who had an area of interest or expertise not included on the list were encouraged to pursue it. Among the topics chosen were Italian opera, the role of women in Italy, and Italy's place in the EEC. Beginning in the third week, students were required to send three postings per week to NEWS, soc.culture.italian. These were written at home so that class time could be spent sending text to the network, checking mail, and discussing other students' postings. (Students read each others work either before or after it was sent to the network.) All the students believed their writing had improved as a result of having communicated through the network. One student stated specifically that she had overcome grammar problems, while the others reported feeling more at ease writing in Italian.

Washington State University graduate student Emmy Pellico describes an elaborate educational research project using the Internet.

- "My first use of telecomputing for this project was my posting to newsgroups asking for literature references that I could review. I did receive some helpful responses to this posting request. In addition, I received two responses from educators in Texas, who were interested in replicating my research in their elementary classrooms. We discussed the research questions, the design, deadlines, samples, limits and boundaries by posting E-mail messages to each other. Through E-mail we agreed to conduct the study and share the results. Before the Texas educators became involved, my own multi-aged kindergarten through second grade sample was very small (only 10). At the same time, a fellow grad student was looking at another sample of 10 students from a multi-aged third-fourth classroom. As my current research continues to progress, we share the data we collect online. We telecommute our progress, questions, and suggestions. In addition to discussing our study, we also add a personal touch by sharing insights about living in our various communities. When we completed our data collection at the end of April, the results of this study were reported in a formal paper in addition to reporting to Washington State University's Department of Education. In preparation for this paper, I performed ERIC searches and used Gopher and Veronica sites to locate related literature on research to review. I have been able to perform all of this work from my home computer at various hours after attending classes, student teaching, and tending my family. Without telecommunications, my research would have been restricted to a small sample, in a particular environment, at a narrow point in time. Because of telecommuting, my research sample increased to become a more credible and valuable contribution to society. Without the convenience of telecomputing from home, my research may have suffered because of conflicting personal priorities. Telecomputing allowed me to work with others who have common research interests collaboratively, globally, efficiently, conveniently, and inexpensively. From the projects that I've participated in and observed, I definitely support the development and enhancement of telecomputing opportunities."

The Internet can often provide immediate and richly detailed information about events in other countries that would not be obtainable in any other way.

- Larry Press, Professor of Computer Information Systems at California State University, Dominguez Hills, experienced first-hand the political might wielded by internetworking during the August 19,1991 Soviet coup attempt. One week prior to the coup, Press co-chaired a conference on human–computer interaction in Moscow. While there, he spent several days visiting the Demos cooperative that operates Reliable Communications (RELCOM), the Russian computer network. Although RELCOM was only a year old in August 1991, more than 400 universities, research institutes, stock and commodities exchanges, news services, high schools, politicians, and government agencies had already joined it. During the conference, Press developed close relationships with the Russians managing RELCOM. At the start of the coup, Press was linked to the Usenet news feed via CSUnet and read a message from his colleague that had been posted in the talk politics.soviet forum of netnews. Vadim Antonov of Demos sent a message that said "I've seen the tanks with my own eyes. I hope we'll be able to communicate during the next few days. Communists cannot rape the Mother Russia once again!" Although the coup leaders had taken over television, radio, newspapers, and all other mass media, they had neglected REL-COM—either as an oversight or because they did not grasp its international reach. This oversight set the tone for RELCOM's activity during the rest of the coup. Antonov's message was quickly and continuously followed by news from various banned Soviet news agencies and government officials. For example, Boris Yeltsin's defiant decrees were carried to Demos headquarters and posted to netnews as soon as they were written. The Russian versions were quickly translated into English and re-posted by several people on the Internet. CNN, AP, and other news agencies were alerted and began watching the postings. Larry responded to Vadim over CSUnet and received the following reply to his first anxious E-mail message from Polina, a Demos staff member. "Don't worry, we're OK, though frightened and angry. Moscow is full of tanks and military machines—I hate them. They try to close all mass media, they stopped CNN an hour ago, and Soviet TV transmits opera and old movies. Now we transmit information enough to put us in prison for the rest of our life (Polina)." Throughout the coup, Russians called in to various RELCOM nodes information that was then posted to the Usenet newsfeed, and RELCOM became the only viable mass communications media operating in Russia. In addition to receiving information from Russia, many people from around the world sent messages to friends and family in Russia. The volume of mail increased so much that Vadim requested that people stop flooding the communications channel. In spite of this volume, Demos did not want to cut off incoming information completely because it was a source of encouragement for the Russians. Press began sending periodic summaries of U.S. news coverage, which Polina translated and posted internally. While this information may have had some value, Press believes that its primary effect was in providing moral support. Afterwards Polina wrote: "You can't even imagine how grateful we are for your help and support in this terrible time! The best thing is to know that we aren't alone. As the coup progressed, the Demos staff realized that they could be shut down or imprisoned and began to disperse their computers and communications equipment so that they could transmit from locations other than their headquarters located within a mile from the KGB headquarters." From Polina came the message "Don't worry; the only danger for us is if they catch and arrest us, as we are sitting at home and distributing the information we have." The operation of RELCOM throughout the coup required great courage since the outcome was uncertain, and the efforts of the Demos staff were acknowledged in the following message posted to talk politics.soviet: "When the dark night fell upon Moscow, RELCOM was one source of light for us. Thanks to these brave people we could get information and hope." The experience of Larry Press provides a shining example of the fact that free communication is incompatible with repressive dictatorship. RELCOM would have been prohibited in the past. Gorbachev's glasnost made RELCOM possible, and it quickly became a significant segment of the Soviet communication infrastructure. RELCOM repaid Gorbachev during the coup by perhaps helping to save his life. Although the coup has ended, the political clout of global computer networks will undoubtedly continue to manifest itself in the future.

The CARL/UNCOVER service, which provides quick access to journal articles and several databases, is rightfully famous. In this piece, Oliver Seely relates his experience with it.

- "In my course Science and Technology I cover a unit about midway through the semester on Controversy in Science. For several years I have been following the debate about the cause(s) of AIDS. There is a group of 40 virologists (now including Luc Montagnier, the discoverer of HIV) who have advanced a compelling argument that there is not yet adequate evidence that HIV is the sole cause of AIDS and perhaps not a cause at all. Journal articles on this subject would be at best difficult to obtain by conventional means, first because I teach in a liberal arts university that does not subscribe to many of the medically oriented journals in which these articles appear, and second because the dispute spills over into many different journals, newspapers, and magazines. A couple of years ago I discovered CARL (The Colorado Alliance of Research Librarians) and its service UNCOVER, a competitor to Current Contents. I can use the service from a standard PC with [a] communications port and it offers powerful keyword search algorithms. It has a singular advantage over the version of Current Contents to which I have access: I can get FAX delivery of an article. The service isn't free; one has either to have a renewable account number, or alternatively, one can enter a Master Card or Visa number for delivery. My half-dozen or so requests up to the present time have arrived at the department FAX machine within 24 hours."

The following story illustrates the potential of the Internet as a unique learning environment where students and NASA experts experiment with designing new types of zero-gravity environments together.

- The Zero-G World Design Project began on May 3, 1991, by Jim Levin at the University of Illinois. Zero-g was a network-based design project in which students and teachers selected an aspect of everyday life and considered how to redesign it to function in a zero-gravity environment. Participants exchanged their designs on the network. The participants in this project worked to construct designs appropriate for a large-scale orbiting zero-g space station. In addition to school children and teachers from around the country, other participants were university researchers, NASA experts, and outside experts. One design challenge was recreation in a zero-g environment. Many novel ideas were presented, which usually were unfeasible at first but evolved through classroom and network communication. One group of fifth graders came up with "roller tennis," which, in their own words ". . . is played on a wooden board with 6 horizontal slits. Inserted in these slits are types of roller skates that look like slippers. Attached to these slipper-like shoes are metal canes in the shape of a 'T.' Wheels are attached on the ends so that the roller skates move sideways and the wheels stay under the board. There is a pair of skates on every slit, 3 pairs on one side facing east and the others facing west. The players move around by 'skating' from side to side and stopping by quickly turning their feet. When a player needs to get closer or farther from the ball, he changes skates." The biggest obstacle in realizing workable designs from this age group was their contextualized understanding of gravity-dependent sports and lack of visualization of what could be possible given the unique characteristics of a space station. The students lacked the scientific background necessary to see why their ideas would not work, but with each iteration of their designs, the knowledge and understanding of the real constraints of the zero-g environment advanced, albeit in small increments. Sometimes, however, these small increments are the result of "giant leaps" in cognition. One such example of these cognitive leaps occurred when one student, Pablo, a member of the roller tennis group, determined that some critical information was needed for their design to evolve. He asked if a tennis ball would move faster in zero gravity and was encouraged to send this question out on the network. Sometimes, as in Pablo's case, it was more important to provide a method for the student to find the answers to critical questions for himself. At other times, collaboration within the classroom was an equally motivating means, especially when two groups hit upon similar ideas. In the pursuit of a space basketball, another group came up with "velcro basketball." During the course of its development, they too made cognitive leaps. This is where Pablo's network exchange was able to lend support. With Pablo's summary of his network messages, the teaching group was aided by one child's newly acquired comprehension of a few scientific principles of zero-g. Zero-g centered on design projects in which students worked independently or cooperatively, performing higher order thinking skills, including problem solving, composition, and reading. Most importantly, zero-g provided a real audience for student writing. Motivation arose from the fact that experts were interested in what they had to say. This is perhaps the most significant aspect of the network's ability to foster a new kind of learning environment, one where children and "experts" communicate to achieve common, real, goals.

Yet another testimony to the value of the Internet in conducting research comes from Dr. Michael Gross of New Jersey.

- "I have found the Internet indispensable to my research. For several years, I have been working with some colleagues in Delaware and Pennsylvania on federally funded ecological/remote sensing research projects. The goals of these projects are to use satellite data to study biogeochemical cycling in wetlands, wetlands vegetation biomass, and temporal changes in wetlands. The benefits of these projects will be an improved understanding of how wetlands affect global ecology, and an ability to understand and monitor man's impacts on wetlands. The projects have been administered through the University of Delaware, and most of the field work has been done in Delaware. Since my colleagues and I teach in colleges and universities, most of our data collection occurs during the summer. We do not have time to analyze the data in the summer. We have been storing our data on a mainframe computer at the University of Delaware. We need a mainframe computer because of the size of the data sets and our need for a powerful statistics package. During the academic year, I have been analyzing the data remotely by using the Internet to access the data files, while physically remaining at my home institution (currently Georgian Court College in New Jersey). By keeping the data in Delaware, all persons in our research group have access to the same data files. The data themselves remain safe within the computer; they cannot become 'lost in the mail,' which could happen if we exchanged hard copies of data files. Also, we have used E-mail on the Internet to communicate about our data. Within the last three years, I have been able to publish the following five peer-reviewed research articles that would have probably not been published without the Internet. I cannot understate the value of a global computer network. It has greatly enhanced my own research productivity."

Finally, not only students, professors, and business people benefit from the Internet's research capabilities. Every one of us can benefit in our everyday as well as our professional lives.

- "This documents an intensely personal use of the Internet. My daughter was scheduled for major surgery in October of 1991 for correction of scoliosis (curvature of the spine). In late summer of that year I decided it was important to learn more about scoliosis. A library catalog search over the Internet led me to discover that another daughter had symptoms, which could mean our family was affected by a serious hereditary disorder known as Marfan Syndrome. A WAIS hypertext search of the database online (mendelian-inheritance-in-man) using the keywords scoliosis and arachnodactyly (long, spidery fingers) suggested an even rarer condition known as Beals Syndrome. The bibliographies found led me to physicians who knew how to diagnose and treat it. The course of treatment became more involved, but had the diagnosis been missed, the consequences would have been very serious. It is not an exaggeration to state that the Internet may have saved my daughter's life!"

Stories of Internet research success abound, often with librarians reporting results that took less time to produce than "it took for the student to explain it to me!" (Karen Schneider, Newark Public Library, 1995, by E-mail). I hope I have succeeded in providing some insights into how the Internet can be useful to you now and in the future. The next section of this book describes the nuts and bolts of using Internet tools and techniques.

Endnotes

1. ABI and YellowNet Partner on Internet Listings. (1995, April 26). Cowles Simba *Media Daily*.

2. Baker, N. (1994, April 4). Annals of Scholarship: Discards. *The New Yorker*, pp. 64–86.

3. Parker, D. B. (1991, October 14). Cited by Glenn Rifkin in "The Ethics Gap." *Computerworld* 25, no. 4, p. 84.

4. Schrage, M. (1995, March). Collaborative Relationships and Virtual Organizations. *Educom Review*, pp. 16–17.

5. Shade, L. (1994, February). Computer Supported Cooperative Work and Academic Culture. *Electronic Journal of Virtual Culture*.

6. Ibid.

3

Using Resources

Power Tools and Internet Research

Once you have decided to use the Internet for a research project, have refined your research question, and have determined what sampling frame and method to use (as outlined in the last section), you need to consider *where* on the Internet the information or people you are looking for can be found. The question of *where* concerns not just the physical location (as in what server at what address in the world of connected computers) but also what tools might be appropriate for locating it. Just as content analysis and survey research have different strengths and weaknesses, so do the various software tools and processes that allow you to navigate the Internet. Each tool does distinct things and can contribute to your work in different ways. It is important to understand these critical trade-offs when developing a research plan involving the Internet.

Because the Internet is so huge, it is not practical to simply browse through the millions of documents that exist on computers scattered around the world, hoping to run into one that has what you need, just as you wouldn't walk into a university library and wander around expecting to bump into a treatise on Dostoyevsky. It is important to have a plan of action when using the Net. However, *unlike* your university library, the Internet has never been cataloged by a trained librarian skilled in categorizing reference materials and creating consistent connections between information and ideas. Although information is freely available on the Net on almost every topic imaginable, it is not organized in any coherent way. In fact, the media description of the Internet as a kind of "information superhighway" is inaccurate because a highway is usually associated with signposts, mile markers, and maps—features the Internet does not have. Consequently, learning how to use the relevant tools, how to evaluate their strengths and weaknesses (and of course, that of the data returned to you), and particularly, how to use the power tips and tricks that Internet experts use will take you a long way toward overcoming the lack of organization on the network.

In this section I focus on the basic techniques each tool requires you to master, with a special emphasis on what I call the true "power research" strategies—the search features that are used by Net experts. Still, even though you may become very skilled at Internet research methods, keep in mind these two caveats:

1. Not everything is on the Internet.

2. A piece of information you need may be on the Internet, but you may not be able to find it, even with the most powerful search engines now available.

If you have an account with Internet access, most of the tools discussed in this section should be available to you. However, wherever possible, I discuss instructions for using each tool by E-mail with just a little extra effort, because some institutions and commercial accounts (such as Prodigy or Compuserve) have limited Internet access, whereas E-mail access is widespread.

Basics of Electronic Mail

Electronic mail, known as E-mail, is a way to send messages or "letters" from one computer to another. Your words are assembled into a form that attaches information about you and your computer system and sends it to a destination you specify. Communicating by E-mail is very inexpensive compared to telephone communication. With E-mail, messages and even files can be exchanged around the world for the cost of a local phone call.

Some reasons why Internet communication is comparatively inexpensive are:

- At various times during the day, networked computers call one another to pick up and transmit mail. Because the long-distance calling areas of computers in geographic proximity to one another overlap (special software makes sure this is always the case), computer systems do not usually have to make a long-distance toll call to make this exchange.

- When an electronic message or computer file is sent over the Internet, the network hardware and software allow multiple files to travel at the same time. That is, because more than one message can be transmitted over the same link at the same time, the overhead cost is dramatically reduced.

- Internet-connected networks lease telephone lines from providers at low rates because of the huge volume of traffic that they generate.

E-mail has many benefits, but perhaps the most powerful is that messages and files sent via E-mail can be downloaded, edited, printed, or otherwise manipulated, unlike faxes or letters. I often send files by E-mail when I am collaborating on a paper, an article, or a proposal, and the recipient can simply add changes to the document and send it back to me, which is very fast and efficient.

Another important feature is that the recipient of an E-mail message can decide when and how E-mail will be read. The telephone has become annoying in many cases because many people feel they must answer it even if it is inconvenient. E-mail provides some flexibility that the telephone does not. Communicating through E-mail is also flexible for senders because there is no need to feel that you are intruding on the time of the people you are sending mail to, because they will **log in** and read their mail at their convenience.

There are many popular E-mail software programs, such as ELM and PINE for shell (UNIX) accounts, and Eudora for SLIP/PPP accounts. Almost all E-mail programs have similar, universal functions. The problem is that all of the E-mail programs use completely different commands to access these functions. Many new users with shell accounts prefer PINE for its easy-to-use menu and online help. Eudora is also user friendly.

Most E-mail programs have one function that will allow you to access and read your incoming mail, another one to save incoming mail in a file, one to print incoming mail, one to send new messages, one to reply to a message, and one to include a file in a mail message or to decode an incoming file attached to a message. Whoever is providing you with an account should have some brief documentation of the E-mail software available to you, with step-by-step instructions. If not, visit your Internet access provider and ask for the following information:

- How to access your E-mail program.

- How to send a new E-mail message.

- How to read an E-mail message someone else has sent to you.

- How to reply to an E-mail message someone else has sent to you.

- How to forward a message sent to you on to someone else.

- How to save an E-mail to a file.

- How to print an E-mail message.

- How to attach a file and to decode a file when sent to you as part of an E-mail attachment.

These basic functions should get you up and running. An additional, more advanced function uses the capabilities of your E-mail program to sort and filter incoming E-mail into manageable categories. For example, you might have a directory into which mail from your mother is automatically placed, one for mail from your girlfriend, and one for mail from classmates and professors. To learn how to use this function, read the documentation for your E-mail program because each one does this a bit differently.

E-mail has the following limitations:

- Do not use E-mail to send a message longer than about 30 pages. Anything longer than that should be compressed (more on this later) and either attached to the E-mail message as a special binary file or transferred using the more efficient FTP.

- It is not generally possible to send text as E-mail *directly* from word-processing software, such as WordPerfect or Microsoft Word, without translating the file to ASCII text. Most word processors include a simple mechanism for converting any file to ASCII text (it will have an extension of .txt), which can then be mailed or uploaded to your shell account for mailing. If you fail to do this, you may be able to E-mail the file, but the recipient will see only an incomprehensible string of characters, not the message you intended to send.

DOMAINS AND ADDRESSES

To send a message on the Internet by electronic mail, you must know the E-mail address. E-mail addresses can be intimidating—some are very long and all seem to be written in some kind of code with strange symbols and spelling—but they can be understood if you know the rules used to create domain names and user names.

Every Internet address has four parts. I will use my E-mail address to illustrate:

charris@ccvax.fullerton.edu

USER NAME AT SERVER NAME(S) DOMAIN

"charris" is typical of the way many E-mail addresses abbreviate or truncate names: c for my first name, Cheryl, and harris, my last name, written as one word. The @ sign (for *at*; usually a shift-2 on the keyboard) tells the computer that the following information will describe where I can be found. "ccvax" is the name of one of my university's servers, the one where most faculty accounts are located, and "fullerton" is my university campus (to distinguish it from the other 20 campuses in the California State University system). Finally, the "edu" at the end makes it clear to others that the user is located at an educational institution.

The server and domain addresses (ccvax.fullerton.edu in this example) are based on something called an **internet protocol (IP) address.**

Each server connected to the Internet has a numerical IP address. The IP address comprises four sets of numbers connected with periods (for example, the IP address for the mail server that I am using at the California State University is 137.151.1.1). Fortunately, these IP addresses can be linked to actual names, which can be remembered more easily than a string of numbers. FTP and Telnet addresses often contain actual IP number strings.

There are several different types of domains, ranging from organization to country codes. A sample of domain types and their references follows:

Domain	Reference
edu	Educational sites in the United States
com	Commercial sites in the United States
gov	U.S. government sites
net	Network administrative organizations

Domain	Reference (continued)
mil	U.S. military sites
org	U.S. organizations (nonprofits, foundations, etc. are often .org domains)
fr	France
ca	Canada
ch	Switzerland
au	Australia
ja	Japan

Each country connected to the Internet has its own country codes. However, many users in other countries are increasingly attracted to the .org or .com domain names, so do not assume that all .com domains you see are U.S. based.

Some E-mail addresses are not reachable via the Internet. If you see an E-mail address that does not conform to the basic four-part address and domain system, it is probably not an Internet network address. Examples of other networks include FidoNet, **BITNET,** MCI Mail, and Genie. It is possible to send mail to some non-Internet addresses through a mail gateway, but you must know how to adapt the address so that Internet-connected servers can get it to the appropriate gateway. Ask the intended recipient for information.

THE E-MAIL ADDRESS AS STATUS SYMBOL

E-mail addresses have become something of a status symbol, identifying the owner as a "card carrying member of the Information Age."[1] Believe it or not, it is thought that ". . . [y]our Net address says volumes about who you are, about what community you hang out in, and whether you are a cybersnob or a cyberhick." Domain names of the major commercial network services, such as @aol.com, @compuserve.com, @prodigy.com, are lowest in the pecking order and are considered less exclusive because they do not provide full Internet access and are open to anyone. Business, educational, and organizational domains (.com, .edu, and .org, respectively) are generally higher in status, although the ultimate in E-mail status is to have your own name as your custom domain name—for example, joe-smith@smith.com. Custom domains cost quite a bit more than other domain names, however, so the status-addicted must pay for the privilege. Universities generally do not make custom domains available to their user base.

THE E-MAIL SIGNATURE

Once you have begun sending and receiving E-mail, you will notice that at the bottom of many E-mail messages is a block of text, often surrounded by graphic characters, that provides contact and other information about the sender. This is known as a signature. For example, a signature might contain the sender's full name, affiliation, telephone number, fax number, and address. Some signatures also contain a sentence or two about the service or business of the sender, or even a quotation from a favorite book, song, poem, or movie. A signature is another way to personalize your correspondence and make it easier for people to get in touch with you.

Some E-mail packages, such as Eudora, make it easy to write a signature file that will be automatically attached to all your outgoing mail. If you have a shell account, however, you will have to manually create a .sig file that will be stored in your account directory. To do this, you need to do one of two things:

1. Use an ASCII text editor (such as Notepad in Windows or Edit in DOS) to write your signature file, save it with the name (.sig), and upload it to your account directory.

2. Use a UNIX text editor (you need to know which ones are available at your site), write the signature file text, and save it as (.sig).

Once you have done this, outgoing mail should automatically include your signature file at the bottom. You can make sure this is working properly by sending a message to yourself. One more note: If you send mail both from a shell account and also from a SLIP/PPP account that goes through the same server, you can end up with double signature files. It is a good idea to disable the SLIP E-mail program signature attachment if this is the case.

Network culture has some preferences concerning the use of signature files, however. It is considered very bad form to use long signature files, because they take up storage space and take extra time. The optimum maximum length of a signature file varies according to the recipient, but in general it is better to avoid creating any signature file longer than four lines. If you use a signature file that is considered to be too long, you can expect flames or at least an occasional protest. Be brief.

If you decide to use a signature file, think it through carefully. In addition to keeping a file short to avoid annoying others, there are also security considerations. If you are sending E-mail to a group of strangers, as in a **Usenet** forum, do you really want to send your telephone number out into **cyberspace** to a potentially unlimited number of people? At the very least, be careful about including your home address or personal identifying information that could be used to harm you. Most people on the Internet are law-abiding citizens, but as in real life, you must protect yourself against the few that may not be so scrupulous.

As for E-mail content, it is best to think first, write later. Because sending E-mail is so easy and fast, it is tempting to toss off messages at the drop of a hat and send them on their way. However, people often live to regret that impulse. E-mail messages, once sent, cannot be recalled. Like any communication, hasty words can come back to haunt you in future years. Remember, too, that electronic communications take on a life of their own and can be saved, forwarded, archived, and otherwise preserved far beyond what you may have intended.

SEARCH STRATEGIES: FINGER, NETFIND, KNOWBOT, WHOIS, ETC.

You want to send someone a message, perhaps a friend back home, and you do not have the E-mail address. What should you do?

Unfortunately, there is no comprehensive global directory of E-mail addresses. The most efficient way to find someone's address is to call on the telephone or send a letter by snail-mail (a pejorative term for the U.S. Postal Service) and ask. If you have already received a message from your friend, you can capture the E-mail address from the header of the message (the few lines at the top of a message that contain the date, sender name, your name, and other information about the travels of the message before it reaches you). Failing that, there are a few limited directory services that might work, but they are not guaranteed. It is estimated that less than 1% of all E-mail users are listed in one of the existing directories, so it is unlikely that you will be able to find the person you are looking for in this manner. Still, it is worth a try. Currently, concerted efforts are underway to build a good database of E-mail addresses, and there are also limited-scope projects, such as the recent *E-mail Addresses of the Rich and Famous,* which contains the private E-mail addresses of celebrities and public figures ranging from Bill Clinton (president@whitehouse.gov) and Bill Gates (billg@ microsoft.com) to Billy Idol (idol@well.sf.ca.us).

Directory search services include Netfind, WhoIs, and Finger. A newer service is Knowbot, an experimental program that does not maintain its own database but goes out and searches databases kept by others.

- *Netfind.* Netfind is useful because it allows you to type in just part of another person's E-mail address and it will try to fill in the rest. Try it by visiting a server running Netfind (your own may do so, so try it first). One server is at

   Telnet: **ds.internic.net** (login as guest)

- *WhoIs*. WhoIs is operated by InterNIC and there are multiple ways to use this program. You can Telnet into InterNIC (address given below) and use the program from there, use the program through a gateway in your **Gopher** program, or send an E-mail request to a WhoIs server (such as InterNIC) with a request to search for you. WhoIs is not very intuitive and has limited abilities.

- *Finger*. **Finger** is a UNIX command that lets you see if someone is logged onto a system at a particular time, and it also grabs any information that might be publicly available about that user. Finger does not help you find an E-mail address, but it will help you find further contact information about a person, if it is accessible (sometimes Finger commands are disabled at a remote site). Use it by typing the command

  finger username@server.domain

(Fill in user name, server, and domain with the proper E-mail address.) The remote system should send back a message with results within a few seconds.

- *Knowbot*. Knowbot will search other databases for you.

  Telnet: **regulus.bucknell.edu 185**

Note that the 185 at the end of the Knowbot server address is the *port* number; it is essential for the remote server to find the precise resource you want.

- *InterNIC White Pages*. The InterNIC organization is responsible for registering new domains and monitoring the overall growth of the Internet. In addition to their many other services, it maintains subject directories of Internet resources and a white pages directory of E-mail addresses. It is not yet close to completion, and it has been criticized as difficult to use, but it is a resource worth trying if all else fails:

  Telnet to: **ds.internic.net**

to see it. While you are there, register your own name by sending an E-mail message to *admin@ds.internic.net* and ask to be added to the white pages directory. (This may or may not work because the system administrators have discretion over who will be added and who will not.)

- *Usenet Posters*. If you think the person you are looking for might have posted something to one of the 10,000+ discussion forums (called Usenet) on the Internet, the E-mail address may be found in a large database maintained at MIT. To initiate a search, send an E-mail message to

mail-server@pit-manager.mit.edu

Do not type anything in the SUBJECT line of the message (or use a blank space if your E-mail program will not send with a blank subject line) and type just one line of text in the message field:

send usenet-address/name

("Name" is the name of the person you are trying to locate.) Within a few minutes you should receive a reply, with either the address you are looking for or a message that the system failed to find the name you specified.

LISTSERVS

E-mail is not limited to one-on-one communication. E-mail can be used to send a single message to many people at once. This capability has been utilized to create a large number of topical discussion groups that distribute the messages of group members through E-mail. There are thousands of these discussion groups, on almost every imaginable subject. Based on the name of the software that facilitates group E-mailing, these private discussion groups are often known as **Listservs**. To receive mail from a Listserv, your must subscribe to it and have the subscription approved by the list group's *moderator*. Although some lists are not moderated, most require a screening process to get your message distributed. In most cases, if you wish to participate in the discussion by sending a message, the moderator will screen the message first and on approval forward it to the rest of the group's membership. Moderators prevent "off-topic" posts from wasting other people's time. Not wasting time and avoiding redundancy are important to mailing list participants. It is considered bad etiquette to send messages to the whole list when you are responding to a single message with a comment such as "good idea" or "thanks for the info. . . ." Such messages should be sent to specific individuals at their private E-mail addresses (easily taken from message headers). Not doing so can invite flames!

The number of existing Listservs is very large and growing larger every day. If you are curious about *all* the possible lists available for subscription, there are several ways to get a comprehensive list.

You can get a list by E-mail. Send a message to

listserv@bitnic.bitnet

with a blank subject line and just one line of message text:

LIST GLOBAL

This will return a huge text file (350 pages or more) that can be downloaded to your word processor and searched. Again, do not keep such large files on the computer network itself. The overall performance of the system suffers if you hog storage space. A better method is to retrieve the file by FTP (details on FTP come later in this section).

The DeSilva List of Lists is available in multiple parts at

rtfm.mit.edu/pub/usenet/news.answers/mail/mailing-lists/Part1...

It is a good idea to avoid jumping right into a discussion list before you are fully cognizant of the climate of the list, the topics that are considered relevant to it, and the expectations of the participants. It is also critical to know how to subscribe, unsubscribe, and otherwise manage your relationship to Listservs.

Perhaps the most important thing about **mailing lists** is that they usually have *two distinct addresses*. One address is for subscribing, unsubscribing, and other administrative functions; the other is for sending messages. Do *not* confuse the two, because list participants get extremely annoyed if they have to read messages asking to subscribe or unsubscribe instead of the pithy insights they expect.

People usually subscribe to a Listserv by using the word *Listserv* in the username field, as in

Listserv@synchro.com

At this domain (synchro.com) is a Listserv that I want to join called JudgeNet. JudgeNet is a mailing list concerned with the "discussion of beer judging and competitions." The synchro.com system is running the Listserv software, but before the Listserv software can subscribe me to JudgeNet, I must tell it who I am and which of its many lists I want to join. To do this I leave the subject line blank and send a message such as

subscribe JudgeNet Cheryl Harris

The Listserv software captures my E-mail address from my header and should send me a message within a few minutes, confirming that I am subscribed to the list or giving the reason why it failed to subscribe me to the list. If the request is successful, keep the confirmation message that is sent back to you because it contains necessary information, such as the procedure for unsubscribing and the address that you must use to post messages to the group.

Listservs tend to be very active, some generating dozens of messages a day. Sometimes you may find that the volume of the list is too high, that the list is not of interest to you, or that you simply need to stop receiving mail for a period of time (such as over the summer or while you are on vacation). To remove yourself from a list, you must *unsubscribe*. Unsubscribe by sending a message to the same address as the one you used to subscribe, with the following message:

unsubscribe JudgeNet Cheryl Harris

Sometimes the Listserv prefers the command *Signoff* to *unsubscribe*, so if one message does not work, try the other.

To rejoin the list at a later date, just repeat the subscription process. Another way to stop mail temporarily is to send the Listserv address a command to halt mail:

set JudgeNet nomail

When you want to receive mail again, you send the command

set JudgeNet mail

Sometimes you may want to receive posted messages posted all at once instead of one message at a time. Many Listserv groups let you request that messages be sent to you in a *digest* form. To do this, send the following message to the Listserv:

set listname digest (where the listname is the name of the discussion list)

Listservs can be a tremendous resource for networking with others who share the same interests as you do, finding experts, and learning about a subject area. However, do not abuse them by dominating a list, harassing participants, or otherwise making a nuisance of yourself. Respect the fact that mailing list participants are involved in the list because it is important for their business or profession or because it concerns an interest or hobby about which they are passionate.

OTHER MAILING LISTS

Some mailing lists use another automated management software called Majordomo, while still others are run manually. Majordomo operates much like Listserv, but instead of sending subscription/unsubscription requests to Listserv, you should send them to Majordomo, as in

majordomo@listname.net

Manually administered discussion groups have only one address, and all mail to the group is read by and acted upon by one person. If you wish to subscribe to one of these, make an effort to be courteous and appreciative of the list owner's efforts.

EMOTICONS

One of the problems with electronic mail is that it is a "flat" communication medium. In other words, people with whom you are communicating through E-mail cannot see your wry smile, see your raised eyebrows, or hear the dripping sarcasm in your voice. The brevity of most E-mail communications also makes them less capable of carrying the kind of descriptive prose that makes a letter emotive. The context of language, much of which is communicated nonverbally, is missing in E-mail. Therefore, your words can be very easily misunderstood. This can lead to inadvertent mistakes that cause flaming.

One way that E-mail users have adopted to try to add "emotion" and nonverbal information to their E-mail messages is with "emoticons" (icons that express emotion). Some E-mail software packages, such as Netmanage's Chameleon, have a standard collection of emoticons built in.

An **emoticon** can be handy when you want to soften a comment:

My paper is going to be a little late, but it will be worth it! :-)

Emoticons are limited by the characters available on a standard computer keyboard, but even so there are hundreds, maybe thousands, of them—dreamed up by inventive users. To "decode" them, tilt your head to the left! A sample of emoticons and their associated meanings follows:

Emoticon	Meaning
:-)	The most basic, a Smiley
:-(	A frown
;-)	A wink
:-|	Indifferent
:-D	Big laugh
%-(	Confused
:-/	Skeptical
:-o	Surprised

ACRONYMS

In addition to using emoticons, Internet users have developed a kind of shorthand that makes extensive use of **acronyms**. Some of the common acronyms that you will see include:

Acronym	Meaning
BTW	By the way

Acronym	Meaning (continued)
\<g\>	Grin (similar to Smiley)
\<vbg\>	Very big grin
LOL	Laughing out loud
ROTFL	Rolling on the floor laughing
TNX	Thanks
BBL	Be back later
CUL8er	See you later
PU	That stinks!
HHOK	Ha, ha, only kidding
IMO	In my opinion
IMHO	In my humble opinion
OTOH	On the other hand
GMTA	Great minds think alike
FYA	For your amusement
FYI	For your information
F2F	Face to face
IOW	In other words
WTG	Way to go

PRIVACY

Be forewarned: E-mail is not private. E-mail is commonly, and incorrectly, assumed to be both impermanent and private. Because E-mail is sometimes written quickly and "on the fly," it is often much more casual, and more frank, than other forms of written communication. E-mail sent through the Internet passes through several gateways (other computer systems) and is archived at the sending and receiving end, sometimes in interim locations as well. Even if you delete a message, and the receiver or sender does too, it can still be recovered from storage archives. In fact, everything you do on a computer system is registered, logged, and traceable. A digital vapor trail is left behind.

The legal industry is already responding to this issue, with companies such as Computer Forensics popping up. Such companies specialize in recovering incriminating electronic evidence in litigation cases.

According to a recent study published in *Macworld* magazine, one in five organizations monitors E-mail messages if there is reason to believe that there is wrongdoing or misuse of resources.[2] Employee awareness programs are now advising workers that "whatever you write on a computer screen can and will be used against you in a court of law."[3]

Although your personal E-mail may not be subject to monitoring, do not take privacy for granted. If you have personal or business communications that must remain confidential, consider encrypting them or sending them by some other, more secure method. Encryption software, such as PGP (Pretty Good Privacy) takes a message and encrypts it using a complex algorithm. The recipient must have the key to decrypt and read the message. PGP encryption is so good that it would take several supercomputers months or years to decrypt a message sent this way. PGP is available in several software archives around the Internet (use Archie to find PGP or use the keyword *encryption* to find other packages).

Encryption has become very controversial. The U.S. government has long been interested in preventing encryption software from becoming widely available because criminals could use it to protect their communications from scrutiny. The author of PGP, Phil Zimmerman, has faced ongoing government investigations since the release of the software. The federal government accused Zimmerman of violating export laws (because the encryption software was made available on the Internet, it was clearly exported worldwide). The battle over PGP may be part of the reason that some software has recently been classified as "munitions" by the U.S. government and thus subject to special regulation. In the past few years, the Clinton administration has attempted to require the installation of something called the Clipper Chip as part of all computers sold in the United States. This would enable the government to decrypt electronic communications. Needless to say, this proposal has been resisted by the computer industry and many others concerned with privacy rights. It is certain that this issue will continue to be important in the coming years.

ANONYMOUS RE-MAILERS

Because of concerns over the lack of privacy with E-mail and the easy identification of E-mail senders, anonymous re-mailing services have developed. These services take incoming mail, strip off the headers that contain the identifying information, and send it on to its destination with "anonymous" in place of the user's name. This service has been the subject of a great deal of debate because someone could harass another Internet user and remain unidentifiable.

STYLE AND ETIQUETTE ISSUES

- *Keep line length short.* Some systems do not wrap text properly, so a rule of thumb is that a line of E-mail text should be no more than 60 characters.

- *Write descriptive subject lines.* A subject line should tell the recipient what the message is about. Avoid cute but unrelated subject lines. The subject line is important because many people are overwhelmed with E-mail messages and make a decision whether to read, save, or delete a message based on the subject line.

- *Avoid writing in ALL CAPS.* Words written in capital letters are considered SHOUTING in Internetese. Besides, upper and lower case letters are much easier to read.

- *Check spelling and grammar.* Be sure your messages are well written. While E-mail messages are frequently informal in tone, they should always have correct spelling and grammar.

- *Emphasize text with *.* Because E-mail messages lack the text-emphasis features of word processors (such as **boldface,** <u>underlining</u>, and *italics*), other means of drawing attention to words are used. The use of asterisks in place of boldface or italics is very common.

    That was a *good* movie.

- *Use sarcasm and humor sparingly.* Remember that E-mail is emotionally flat and that sarcasm and humor work well only in conjunction with body language, intonation, and other nonverbal cues. Be careful about using these in E-mail messages because your meaning may be misunderstood.

- *Forwarding.* Do not forward or redirect someone else's message without permission, because it is impossible for you to be certain whether or not doing so might cause the original sender harm.

- *Use a short signature.* Remember to keep your signature at or under four lines.

There are even guidelines for flaming. As I said earlier, a flame is an "inflammatory remark or message . . . that contains insensitive language or impetuous negative responses."[4] Because of the one-dimensionality of E-mail as a communication medium, meanings can be easily misunderstood. Disagreements flare up and become very important for a brief period, creating a flame war. It is best to avoid firing an angry message if a discussion becomes heated, but if you must, try to ask yourself if you would say the same thing if you were face to face with the person. Often, you will find you would not.

FAX SERVICES AVAILABLE THROUGH E-MAIL

Faxes that will print on the recipient's fax machine can be sent around the world by E-mail. There are two kinds of services: free services and services where faxes are delivered for a fee. If you are working on a project, such as a job search, in which faxes are to be sent over long distances, this service can save a great deal of money because sending faxes through E-mail does not incur long-distance telephone charges. If you do not have access to a fax machine and need to send faxes, the service can be a lifesaver.

- *Free fax service by E-mail*: A free experimental service with limited geographic coverage is available. To learn more, send mail to

    tpc-faq@town.hall.org

    and you will receive a copy of the Internet FAQ for FAX services list.

- *Fee-based fax service*: Interfax is worldwide, but it costs $5 a month. For further information, send E-mail to

    faxmaster@pan.com

MAILING LIST ARCHIVES

Many mailing lists also maintain archives, so if you are interested in a mailing list topic but do not want to receive regular mail, you can visit their archive. These archives are made available by Gopher or WWW, and information about how to reach the archive is usually part of the confirmation message sent upon subscription. Also, an Archie, WAIS, or Webcrawler search using the mailing list name should turn up an archive site if one exists.

Usenet

The Usenet is very similar to the Listserv groups discussed in the previous section. Both run under E-mail, and both are concerned with topical discussions on professional or leisure topics. The difference between Listservs and the Usenet is that Usenet messages are not delivered to the recipient's mailbox. Instead, the user's computer system periodically downloads a feed of the Usenet groups needed by users at that site, and the user must also launch special newsreader software to browse the groups and read new messages or "posts" (see Figure 2).

F I G U R E   2

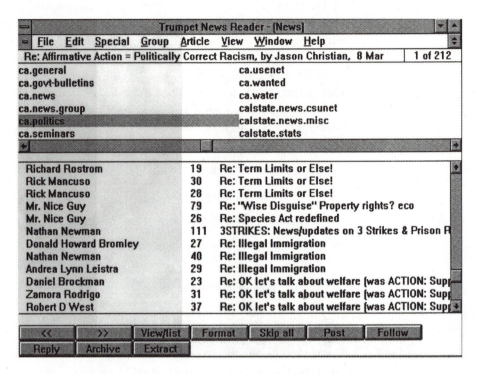

There are more than 10,000 Usenet groups, and they are organized in a hierarchical scheme by type of content. There are many categories, but the most popular are:

comp	computer-related topics
sci	science topics
rec	recreational topics
alt	alternative topics, some of questionable taste
misc	miscellaneous topics (also those that cross topical boundaries)
talk	debate-oriented discussion
news	issues surrounding Usenet and discussion forums
biz	business and commercial issues
soc	social issues discussion

These categories precede a more extended description of the specific group theme. For example, here are three Usenet groups:

comp.sys.amiga.audio
comp.sys.amiga.advocacy
comp.sys.amiga.applications

All three of these groups are located in the computer hierarchy (comp.). All three are concerned with systems, and all three are for Amiga enthusiasts. However, it is easy to see by looking at the last part of the group names that each one deals with a different aspect of Amiga computer systems: one is for audio issues, another for advocacy, and the last one is for various Amiga applications.

Most of the **client** software used to read Usenet groups makes it fairly easy to subscribe, unsubscribe, mark and print messages, and perform other functions. In a shell account, the most popular newsreader is *tin*, and these three letters are usually enough to launch the newsreader software.

POWER USES

Like mailing lists, Usenet discussion forums gather experts, authorities, and interested people for a huge variety of topics. For a researcher, this is an important resource where the potential for learning is unparalleled. Usenet makes it possible to quickly find the right person to ask a particular question—on over 9,000 topics.

BASICS

Commands necessary to perform basic Usenet functions differ depending on the newsreader you are using. Usenet news cannot be read without newsreader software, running on either your PC or on the remote computer system. However, most newsreaders will have a command summary at the bottom or top of the screen that will remind you what to do.

In *tin*, the command summary is at the bottom of each screen. In a SLIP/PPP newsreader such as Trumpet Newsreader, there are always a menu at the top and buttons along the bottom of each screen so that commands are a matter of pointing and clicking.

For the particular newsreader that you will use, gather documentation on the following areas:

- *How to access your Usenet reader*: Tin can usually be started from the system prompt in your shell account with the word *tin*. If this does not work, your system is using another software (such as nn or trn) or a Usenet newsreader is not available on your system.

With Trumpet Newsreader, the Winsock software must have an active connection (see the section on configuring and running SLIP/PPP accounts and Winsock later in this chapter) before you can launch the Newsreader by double-clicking on its icon.

- *How to access or subscribe to a particular newsgroup*: The first time you run the tin newsreader software from within your account, you will be presented with a long list of **newsgroups** and asked to confirm whether or not you wish to subscribe to each one of them. Alternately, you may subscribe manually by typing in the appropriate subscribe command and the group name (look at the command summary for details). The next time you log in, the groups to which you are subscribed will be listed, and you will be able to move between them, reading any messages you like.

  With the Trumpet Newsreader, subscribing to a group is very simple and is done by choosing the Subscribe command from the top menu, which presents a screen with a scrollable list of news-group hierarchy names (from a to z). You simply click on groups in which you are interested and they are placed in the "subscribed" area of the screen.

- *How to unsubscribe to a particular newsgroup*: You can unsub-scribe to a group at any time, and all newsreaders make this a fairly simple procedure. Other things that you can do include "catching up" on messages, which clears messages you may or may not have read and presents you with a clean slate. The next time you log in you will be shown only messages that have arrived since the catch-up command.

Each newsreader has a slightly different command structure for accomplishing each of these basic procedures. See your system administrator for specific instructions on how to use the newsreader software provided for you. However, make sure you understand from the instructions how to do each of the following, in addition to subscribing and unsubscribing:

- How to read a post.

- How to send a post.

- How to save a post.

- How to move from one newsgroup to another.

- How to exit your Usenet reader.

FREQUENTLY ASKED QUESTIONS FILES (FAQS)

FAQs are easy to find and must be read before you jump into a group discussion. Periodically the FAQ for a group will be posted as a message. You should also be able to find it in the group

    news.answers

Quite a few FAQs are available through the WWW, which you will learn to use shortly.

STYLE AND ETIQUETTE

Etiquette on Usenet is similar to the guidelines for E-mail and Listserv. Many articles have been posted to Usenet newsgroups discussing Usenet news etiquette (or "netiquette"). Before you start posting to a public Usenet newsgroup, you should become familiar with its netiquette and the netiquette of Usenet newsgroups in general. One rule of thumb is to subscribe to a newsgroup for a certain amount of time and read many of the discussions that take place to observe the "culture" of the particular newsgroup. You will soon learn the difference between an acceptable post and an unacceptable post. You should also read the FAQ for that newsgroup before you begin posting. This will help you avoid a situation where you ask a question that has been asked frequently in the past. That is one of the many crimes, along with blatant advertising or junk posts, that generate flaming.

There are Usenet resources that answer questions about how Usenet works. The best of these are

- *news.answers*: This newsgroup is the first place to look for a group's FAQ.

- *news.newusers.questions*: This is a place where you can ask question about Usenet protocol, etc.

- *news.announce.newusers*: This group has technical information on Usenet.

SEARCH STRATEGIES

WAIS and some WWW search engines will search Usenet news for certain topics and keywords. Another important tool that may help you find particular items of interest is the Stanford Netnews Filtering Service. This service creates a personalized delivery system for you, searching all Usenet news postings for items that match a profile you have instructed the system to follow. The profiles are in plain text and do not allow Boolean (AND, OR, NOT) operations. It can be accessed by a WWW **browser** at

http://woodstock.stanford.edu:2000

E-mail access to the Stanford Netnews Filtering Service is also available. Instructions can be received by sending an E-mail message with only the word *help* in the message body to

netnews@db.stanford.edu

USENET AVAILABLE BY E-MAIL

Some systems do not carry Usenet feeds because of insufficient storage, fear of liability, or other concerns. However, you may post to Usenet by E-mail and then keep up with responses by checking the archives periodically. Post to any discussion group by replacing the periods (.) in the group name with a dash (-) and using one of two servers:

groupname@cs.utexas.edu
groupname@pw.bull.com

For example, comp.sys.amiga.audio would become *comp-sys-amiga-audio@cs.utexas.edu*. Then type the post in the body of the message and send the mail.

Internet Relay Chat (IRC)

E-mail, Listservs, and Usenet are useful ways to communicate, but they suffer from being strictly asynchronous. There is a significant time lag between sending a message and receiving a reply. This can be inefficient if the task at hand is time sensitive. However, there are also several real-time services that allow people to talk to each other without delayed responses. Internet Relay Chat (IRC) is one of these. Like Usenet, IRC is organized into many special interest groups (called *channels*), but the difference is that these groups are not fixed by name or topic. As a result, IRC is a very fluid medium, constantly evolving and changing depending on who is online.

Much has been written about IRCs and other chat forums' unique environments. Because interacting in cyberspace means that others cannot see you, it is possible to assume an entirely new identity and to change identities at will, something that is difficult or impossible to do in real life. Consequently, there is a great deal of experimentation on IRC with gender switching and sexuality. Amorous online adventures are known as "**lofting**,"[5] and the anonymity of interactive chat environments such as IRC have been known to lessen inhibitions in interesting ways. Fantasies can be acted out: Gay men can become heterosexual, men can become women, and women can be men—at least for the time they are online.[6]

There are unknown social implications from such activities, and from computer-mediated communication in general, both because of its "ability to overthrow centralized control of information to its potential ability to help people, no matter what their gender, race, or physical appearance, communicate with each other with fewer prejudices and misunderstandings than any other medium in existence."[7]

Recently there has been an increase in people "marrying online," becoming virtual or online husbands and wives. Lofters insist that this activity is harmless and does not endanger their real-life relationships. Although most lofters do not meet each other in real life, and in fact may live continents apart, some do pursue their online relationships. American talk show host Rush Limbaugh met his current wife in a chat forum on Compuserve.

The potential of IRC for exploring dimensions of human communication, relationships, roles, and sexuality is enormous.[8] However, it is also a powerful productivity tool.

POWER USES

IRC has a number of functions of use to researchers and students. Although it is used primarily for recreational chat, it is sometimes used to conduct interviews, hold conferences between offices or colleagues, and more recently, as a conduit for live telephone conversations using the new Internet Phone software. Many users report that IRC is also a continuous support group, available 24 hours a day around the world. There are already several professional psychiatrists and therapists who use IRC or other interactive chat environments to treat patients.[9]

Because IRC is a global interactive forum and therefore crosses time zones and geographic boundaries, no matter what time it is, there is always someone online who wants to talk.

BASICS

If you need to converse by keyboard with a classmate or professor logged in to the same computer system as yours, then you should be able to use an interactive program called TALK, which sets up a two-way real-time connection, like a telephone call. However, IRC is more flexible because it allows many people to engage in the same discussion interactively and in real time. On IRC, you join a channel on a topic of interest to you, and whatever you type is instantly broadcast to everyone on that channel. A few minutes ago, as I took a break from writing this, there were 653 active channels and about 2,200 people on IRC.

Your local computer system may not have access to IRC, although most systems do. You can find out quickly by logging in to your server and typing *IRC* or by asking your system administrator. If you wish to run IRC from a SLIP/PPP account, you need to obtain the IRC II client software (search for it with Archie); this is shareware (software that you are able to evaluate and pay for only if you decide to use it) and widely available.

Using IRC requires making a few decisions. First, you must select a *nickname* that you will use to identify yourself during the IRC session. Second, once online you must select one of the available channels to *join*. All conversation on IRC takes place on a channel; you cannot participate without joining one.

When first logging in to IRC, you are placed in the NULL or ZERO channel and cannot participate in any discussions yet. When you log in, give yourself a nickname by typing

/nick *nickname*

Replace *nickname* with your desired name for the session. You can change this nickname later in the session if you wish, but until you do, this is how you will be identified.

The / is very important and must precede all commands in IRC. Without it, IRC will not recognize what you type as an instruction.

Next, you want to choose a channel. At any time, there will be *many* available to choose from. A complete list can be reviewed by typing

/list

Because there can be hundreds of channels available online at one time, the list command may cause a bewildering scroll of channel names across your screen, and it may happen too quickly for you to be able to read the names. A large number of these channels consist of single users, who just set up channels on particular topics and wait for someone else to happen by who wants to talk about that particular topic too. It is possible to reduce the size of the channel list by typing

/list -min *n*

n is the minimum number of people within the channel that you want to see; 2 is a good minimum. Alternatively, replace -min with -max if you wish to set an upper limit to the number of people in a channel for you to be notified of it.

Each channel name is preceded by the # sign and followed by the number of people who are currently participating in that channel's discussion. A few channels have thoughtfully provided a description of the channel's topic(s) next to the name (too bad more do not do this!). You can see the nicknames (not the real names) of others who have joined a particular channel by typing

/names *#channelname*

Replace *channelname* with the name of the channel, i.e., *politics* or *hottub*. Search for a channel name with a particular pattern or topic by typing

/list *comput*

This wildcard (* is a wildcard character) search should return a list of any current IRC channels with the word computer, computing, or computers in their names, including variants such as computation.

When you are ready to join a channel, type

/join *#channelname*

Replace *channelname* with the name of the channel, i.e., *politics* or *hottub*.

When you are in a channel, everything you type will be seen by everyone else who has joined that channel, including your nickname. You can send private messages, but only with the following command:

/msg *nickname* message-text

Replace *nickname* with the name of the user you want to send the private message to, and replace message-text with the actual message. As you can guess, private messages on IRC should remain fairly short.

To leave a channel, simply type

/leave *channelname*

Once you become comfortable with joining and leaving channels, you can join several channels at once and monitor and/or participate in their discussions by typing the command

/set novice off

If you are using IRC to conduct a conversation or interview with a specific person and you log in before they do, you need to set up the channel that you will use. Agree before the session on the channel name, however, so that the other person or persons will be able to find your channel. Channels are created by using the join command, and supplying the new channel name, as in

/join *#interview*

Interview is the channel name chosen.

IRC will create a new channel called #interview, assuming there is no other active channel by that name. If there is, you will simply be joined to it, and you can leave and create another new channel. The creator of a new channel becomes the *channel operator* and as such has special privileges. A channel operator can designate that the new channel will become private, secret, moderated, by invitation only, or restricted in other ways. Channel operators can be recognized because IRC places an @ sign in front of their nicknames. Channel operators set channel restrictions with the /mod command (see the online help for more details on /mod).

IRC has online help available at any time, which you access by typing /help.

If you need help on a specific command, type the command also, as in

/help join

This message will return help information on how to join a channel.

When you are ready to leave IRC, one of the following two commands allows you to leave it.

/quit or /signoff

Figure 3, an example of a fairly innocuous discussion on the #WWW channel, illustrates how the system announces newcomers as well as those who sign off the channel as the discussion progresses.

FIGURE 3 EXAMPLE OF AN IRC DISCUSSION

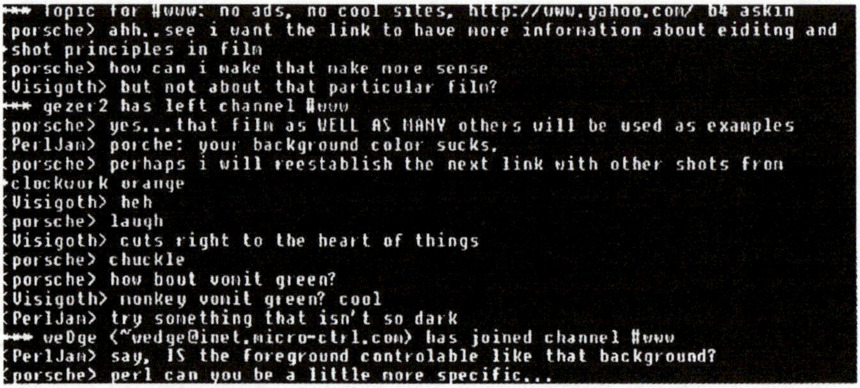

```
*** Topic for #www: no ads, no cool sites, http://www.yahoo.com/ b4 askin
<porsche> ahh..see i want the link to have more information about eiditng and
shot principles in film
<porsche> how can i make that make more sense
<Visigoth> but not about that particular film?
*** gezer2 has left channel #www
<porsche> yes...that film as WELL AS MANY others will be used as examples
<PerlJan> porche: your background color sucks.
<porsche> perhaps i will reestablish the next link with other shots from
clockwork orange
<Visigoth> heh
<porsche> laugh
<Visigoth> cuts right to the heart of things
<porsche> chuckle
<porsche> how bout vomit green?
<Visigoth> monkey vomit green? cool
<PerlJan> try something that isn't so dark
*** wedge (~wedge@inet.micro-ctrl.com) has joined channel #www
<PerlJan> say, IS the foreground controlable like that background?
<porsche> perl can you be a little more specific...
```

SBOTS, LURKING, AND OTHER IRC PHENOMENA

Bots   A bot (short for robot) is an automated script that searches for and returns information to the bot launcher. They are the forerunners of "smart agents" that automate many tasks. Bots have a lot of potential for good, but they have been used on IRC and elsewhere for antisocial or negative purposes. Some heated or controversial discussions on IRC make people wish they could stop some people from contributing their two cents' worth. Such annoyances resulted in the creation of a software code with just that capability; this type of software is known as Cancelbots. Most IRC operators ban the use of any kind of bots on their systems, and there can be severe repercussions for using bots.

Lurking   When someone joins a channel but does not participate in the discussion, it is known as **lurking.** Others know there are *lurkers* because the system makes an announcement every time someone joins a channel and leaves it. There is nothing wrong with lurking, particularly if you are simply trying to ascertain whether or not the topics under discussion are relevant to you and how to participate in keeping with the prevailing cultural norms. However, occasionally lurkers get scolded by discussants who object to being "spied upon."

Nickserv   If you expect to spend quite a bit of time on IRC on a regular basis, you may want to take steps to protect your nickname from being used by others. This is useful for frequent visitors because others will get to know you by your nickname. While channel names cannot be protected, the most popular ones are *always* active, because there is always someone in some part of the world inhabiting the channel.

Protect your nickname by registering with the Nickserv robot program. If someone else signs in to IRC with your unique nickname, Nickserv sends that user a warning (but does not prevent its use, if the person logging in insists on it). Still, most users are considerate of unique nicknames and choose another one after a Nickserv warning. If you do not log on with your nickname within an eight-week period, however, Nickserv will let the nickname warning expire. To get more information, type the following message from within IRC:

/msg Nickserv@service.de help

STYLE AND ETIQUETTE

IRC discussions can move very quickly, and because they occur in real time and interactively, it is easy to let considerations of style and etiquette fall by the wayside. Remember that errors in punctuation, spelling, and grammar make your meaning harder to decipher.

Moreover, IRC discussions are just as prone to flaming or mailbomb-ing as any other discussion medium on the Internet, so you must be as considerate on IRC as you are elsewhere on the network.

File Transfer Protocol (FTP)

File transfer protocol (FTP) is a method for transferring files between computer systems, even computer systems of different types that would otherwise be incompatible with one another. FTP is useful when you need a copy of a document or need to retrieve a file, such as a piece of software stored on a remote system. FTP allows users from outside systems to log in as "anonymous" guests and visit only the area containing public files, copying any that they want to their own PC hard drive or server drive. Although the procedure is called **Anonymous FTP**, it isn't. The remote system logs your account address and what you do when you are on the system (see Figure 4).

F I G U R E   4

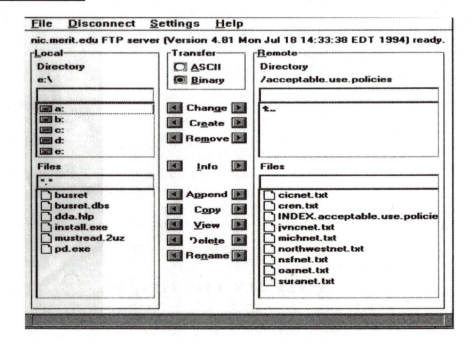

POWER USES

FTP is a fast and efficient method of file transfer, capable of exchanging far larger files than would be possible via E-mail. Many, if not most, of the informational treasures on the Internet are accessible through Anonymous FTP, including databases, photos and images, data archives, recipes, software, and millions of other documents and files.

Researchers make extensive use of FTP, usually searching for and retrieving specific files from FTP servers or exchanging large files between project collaborators.

BASICS

To use FTP you must know the *location* of the files you want (see Figure 5). FTP, unlike tools such as Gopher or the WWW, does not permit browsing outside each individual system. Consequently, learning how to use search tools such as Archie is very important. Otherwise, with millions of FTP servers connected to the Internet, it could take several lifetimes to log on and log off individual systems, one after another, trying to find a specific file. Other sources for finding files available by FTP are the

FIGURE 5

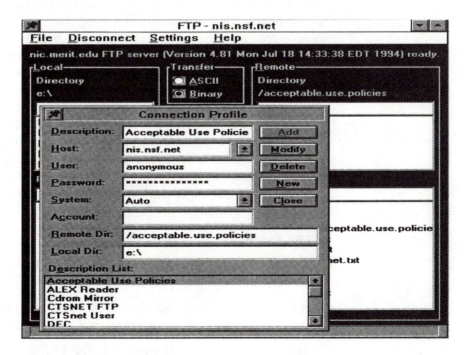

popular annual guides to Internet sites, such as Hahn and Stout's *The Internet Yellow Pages* and Rutten's *Netguide*. These guides organize all kinds of resources by subject and provide location information. There are also several extensive online directories organized by subject heading, category, server, or topic. Some pointers to these are contained in Part 4. The exact location of an FTP site and file will look much like this:

> server & domain names/directory/subdirectory/filename.ext

For example, I have a GIF file (a graphic) available on an FTP server with the following location:

> ftp.cts.com/pub/charris/blueline.gif

This is a *path* statement, which will look familiar to you if you are a DOS or Windows user. It describes a file nested within a directory structure on a particular server. The file you are looking for is often inside a directory called *pub* and possibly another subdirectory below that.

FILE COMPRESSION AND DECOMPRESSION SOFTWARE

Files are given at least a three-letter *extension* that conveys information about the type of file it is or how the file has been compressed and what you will need to do to *uncompress* it. Files are compressed to save storage space. The most popular compression software you will encounter are PKZIP and PKUNZIP. PKZIP compresses software (.zip as an extension indicates that the file has been compressed with PKZIP), whereas PKUNZIP is used to uncompress software once it has been downloaded to your computer. Both PKZIP and PKUNZIP are available from many software archives by FTP (run Archie to find it). Other extensions you may see include .arc, .z, .tar, and .gzip. For each of these, you need to find the corresponding decompression software, which is usually easily available in software archives under the extension name or in directories called *compress* or something similar.

File Extension	Meaning
.txt	An ASCII, plain text file; needs no decompression
.gif	An image in the graphics interchange format; requires special viewer software
.zip	Compressed with PKZIP; needs PKUNZIP to uncompress it

.Z	Compressed with COMPRESS software; needs UNCOMPRESS to read it
.z	Compressed with PACK; needs UNPACK to read it
.gz	Compressed with GZIP; needs GUNZIP to read it
.tar	Indicates a compressed UNIX file or software, rarely of use to PC users because system administrators are unlikely to allow you to run on their systems software that you install yourself. Always ask permission if you need to run something on a UNIX system that the sysadmin did not provide.
.uue	A file compressed with the UNIX UUENCODE program; requires UUDECODE to read it

LAUNCHING FTP

Run FTP either by typing FTP at your system prompt (within a shell account) or by double-clicking on the FTP icon from your SLIP/PPP account. First be sure the Winsock is running in the background and you are connected to the server properly. The system will prompt you for the address of the system to which you wish to be connected.

For example, to get the file I mentioned earlier from my FTP directory, you would first type in the address:

ftp.cts.com

Then you must wait for the system to try to connect you.

Sometimes the system has too many users already logged in, and if this is the case you should get a message back saying something like "login refused." This is nothing personal; it simply means you should try again later. Another kind of error message is "host not found," which usually signals that you have mistyped the address of the remote system. Remember that UNIX systems are case sensitive and rather literal creatures, like all computers. Try to establish the connection again, carefully typing the name exactly as it is written. If the "host not found" error is returned again, it may mean that the server is no longer public, that the FTP function has moved to another server, or that you have made a mistake writing down the address and need to look it up again.

If the remote system is available for use, you will be prompted for your user ID or user name. In this case, always respond anonymous

Next, you will be prompted for your **password**. This is always your account address; in my case, I would type

charris@ccvax.fullerton.edu

If all went well, you should see a message on your screen confirming that you are logged in to the remote system.

With a SLIP/PPP account, the procedure is slightly different, because the FTP client requires that a connection profile be filled out for each target system before an attempt to connect is made. The connection profile includes how you want to log in, your password, and which directories you want the system to find once it connects. It automates several of the steps that must be performed manually when you are running an FTP session with a shell account.

GETTING THINGS DONE

When you are sure that you are properly logged on to the remote system, you must move to the directory or subdirectory containing the file that you want. With a SLIP/PPP account, this is as simple as pointing and clicking with the mouse, but if you have a shell account, you must master some UNIX and FTP commands.

Navigating through the directories requires the use of a few basic commands:

Command	Action
cd	Change directory (tunnels deeper into the file structure)
cdup	Change directory upwards (to the next directory above the one you are in)
dir	See a directory listing of files

For example, when you first log on to retrieve my file *blueline.gif*, you are by default in the *root* directory of ftp.cts.com. To get to the file, you must move through two other directories, the subdirectory of the root directory called *pub* and the subdirectory of pub called *charris*.

Here is how it looks:

ftp.cts.com   You are logged in as xxxxxx@xxxxx.xxxx
xxxxxx root directory xxxxx

If no directory name is listed, type *pwd* to find out where you are.

Step 1. To see a list of all directories under the root, type *dir*. The result might be:

```
pub      dir
misc     dir
private  dir
papers   dir
```

Step 2. In this case there are four directories to choose from. You know you need to be in the *pub* directory first, so you type

cd pub

(Be sure to press the ENTER key on the keyboard each time you want the computer to process a command; otherwise, it will not recognize that you are finished typing.)

To see if you are now within the pub directory, you can ask for a directory listing again by typing

dir

Don't forget to press the ENTER key after the command. The result is

```
xxxx pub xxxxxxx          arthur   dir
                          mable    dir
                          charris  dir
                          john     dir
                          carol    dir
                          paul     dir
                          evelyn   dir
```

Step 3. You are in the *pub* directory, and there are 7 subdirectories here, including *charris,* the one you are looking for. To get there, type

cd charris

Next, you want to see if the file you want is in the charris directory, so you ask for a directory listing again by typing

dir

The result is

```
xxxx charris xxxxxxx      yellow.gif
                          blueline.gif
                          redline.gif
```

Yes! There it is—*blueline.gif.*

TRANSFERRING FILES

Now that you have found *blueline.gif* you need to begin the transfer process. The next command you type will depend on the file extension information. If the file extension of the file you want is anything other than .txt (for plain ASCII text), it is probably a binary file, which means that if it is to be transferred successfully it requires special error checking procedures. All software is binary, and any file that has been compressed is binary. Since ASCII or .txt files can be transferred by FTP just without problems with either binary or ASCII mode, it is safe to tell the computer you wish to use the BINARY transfer process. Do this by typing

binary

at the command prompt. The computer will return a message saying that the file type has been reset to binary (or I for image). Once this occurs, you are ready to instruct the computer to begin the transfer.

To retrieve a single file, type

get blueline.gif

You should receive a message saying the transfer was successful. To get all the .gif files in the directory, type

mget *.gif

The *mget* command "gets" multiple files at once; here you use a wildcard to tell the computer to get all the files ending with the extension .gif. Note that both mget and wildcards must be used prudently to avoid retrieving files you do not want along with those you do. While FTP transfers are fast, large files can take a long time to transfer and tie up your computer for longer than you may want.

With a shell account, once files have been transferred to your directory with get or mget, suppose you want to move files in the opposite direction, from your directory to the FTP server on another computer system. Note that most FTP servers do not allow "uploads" from users, or they do so only with restrictions. Make sure you have permission to upload before attempting to do it, especially since many people must pay additional fees to store files over a certain size limit.

To send a file to another system, you must know the exact location of the destination directory. The log on procedure is identical, and you must navigate down to the target directory as though you were retrieving a file or files.

You want to send the file *cheryl.zip* to a friend. Once you reach your friend's computer system's FTP server and the proper directory, the command is

put cheryl.zip

This command "puts" the file in the target directory. If you have many files to send, you can use the following variant:

mput *.zip

This sends all files in your local directory with the extension .zip to your friend. Convenient, isn't it?

Online help is available on most FTP servers, simply by typing *help* at the prompt.

To leave a system, you use the commands *close* and *exit*. Be sure to properly log off the remote system, and your own account, at the end of the session.

NETIQUETTE

FTP servers that allow outside, anonymous access are not usually devoted exclusively to that service. Consequently, high traffic or other problems on the FTP part of the server can disrupt or even crash other activities taking place on the nonpublic part of the server. It is simply good common sense to avoid creating problems for people trying to get work done, and the best way to do this is to schedule downloads of large multiple files for off-peak hours, outside the working day (you need to pay attention to the local time wherever the remote server is). Servers usually try to prevent excess traffic by limiting the number of simultaneous users, which is why it sometimes takes several tries to get logged in to popular sites (such as any of the software archives). It is also expected that remote FTP users will log in with the complete account address in the password field, even though FTP servers log this information automatically.

ESTIMATING CONNECT TIME

During an FTP session, you can obtain information about files by requesting a directory listing, which usually includes information about file sizes, the date each file was uploaded, and so on. File size in particular is relevant for two reasons:

1. If you have a shell account, storage space on the system you are using is limited. Large files should be very important to you to justify downloading them, and you should move these files to your own hard drive, erasing them from the server as soon as possible. Keep in mind that large files may also take a long time to move from the server to your PC, depending on the speed of your **modem.**

2. If you have a SLIP/PPP connection, the time required for a file transfer depends on the speed of the modem you are using and the size of the file. Even with a very fast modem (14.4 baud and above per second), files of more than a **megabyte** or two can take a

painfully long time, tying up system resources and trying your patience as well. You may have to calculate manually the amount of time it may take to transfer a file, but some systems will estimate it . for you. Take the time to find out, because it is not always easy to abort a transfer once it is underway.

You can roughly estimate the connect time by dividing the speed of your modem by 10—the number of characters the modem can handle per second. Check the file size of the file you want in bytes, and divide it by the previous number, which will give you an estimate of the number of seconds. Divide this number by 60 to get the number of minutes required for the transfer—usually more than you expect unless you have a very fast connection.

For example, Karen has a 2400 baud modem and the file she wants is 87500 bytes.

$2400/10 = 240$

$87500/240 = 365.6$ seconds

$356.6/60 = 5.9$ minutes

The file she wants should transfer in 5.9 minutes. This does not include time needed for errors, retries, or other problems.

MIRRORS

Popular sites are frequently overloaded with users and it is difficult to log on. To accommodate the Internet community, some sites thoughtfully provide a *mirror* of themselves. A mirror duplicates the files available on a specific FTP site on yet another site. The locations of alternative, or mirror, sites are usually announced at the time that a remote system sends a "failure to logon" message due to too much traffic. Mirrors are often much less crowded and are always worth a try.

SEARCH STRATEGIES

As I mentioned earlier, to make the Internet's vast stores of information work for you, you must be able to find what you need efficiently and quickly. To do so requires learning how to use the best available search tools and directory resources.

Archie   For finding specific files, **Archie** (see Figure 6) is always my first stop. Archie is both a software program and an associated database. The software regularly polls known FTP sites not on the Internet and retrieves copies of the directory lists in the public FTP areas. Archie then stores these lists in its database, so that it is searchable by you. Many servers around the world run the Archie software and allow outside users to search their Archie database. Your own server may run it; you may need to ask the system administrator about it.

Archie, like all other search mechanisms currently available on the Internet, is not foolproof. One problem Archie faces is that people can give files on FTP servers whatever names they want, whether or not they are relevant descriptions of the contents of the file. So, if you tell Archie to find files containing census data, it is possible that Archie cannot tell you about such files if the files do not have the word *census* in their file names. There is also a time lag between Archie polls, so very recent files may not be represented in the Archie database when you search it. Note that you cannot FTP to Archie.

FIGURE 6 ARCHIE

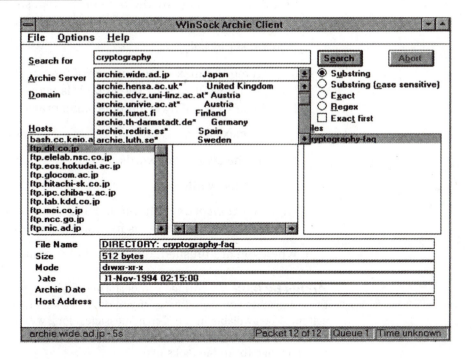

There are four ways to access Archie:

1. Use Archie on your local server if it is running the Archie software.

2. Send commands to an Archie server by E-mail asking it to search for you and E-mail back the results.

3. Use a process called Telnet to move to a remote server running Archie and search the database there.

4. Use a process called Gopher to move to a remote server running Archie and search the database.

Running Archie   The steps for performing a search using Archie are as follows:

1. From your local server, or from a remote server you have reached with Telnet or Gopher, log in as *archie.*

2. Instruct Archie that you want it to search by both directory and filename by typing

   set search sub

3. Tell Archie how you want it to sort the results of your search. I prefer to see results by the date of the file, so that I can choose the most recent files.

   set sortby time

4. Tell Archie the maximum number of file names that match the criteria you want to see. The default is usually 100, but it is preferable to set a lower number. I generally use 25 or fewer.

   set maxhits 25

5. Provide the search keywords

   prog keywords

   (Replace *keywords* with the filename or other descriptor for which you are searching, as in prog Macintosh.)

6. When you are finished, quit with the *q* command.

Archie by Mail   Archie can perform searches by E-mail. However, all of the commands you would enter if you did a search on an Archie server yourself must be available in the E-mail message, along with the instructions about where you want Archie to send the results. Here is an example of what an E-mail message to Archie looks like.

   set mail to username@server.domain

(Replace username@server.domain with your address.)

   set maxhits n

(Replace n with the maximum number of file names you want to see, and set it low.)

```
set search sub
set sortby time
prog filename
q
```

Telnet Accessible Archie Servers   Information on how to use Telnet
remote computing resources is discussed later in this section. However, here
are addresses of Archie servers and their Telnet addresses:

Address	**Country**
archie.sura.net	USA
archie.rutgers.edu	USA
archie.internic.net	USA
archie.hensa.ac.uk	UK
archie.funet.fi	Finland
archie.au	Australia

Other resources for finding FTP sites include the following directories:

- *Macintosh FTP List.* This is a specialized list of FTP sites relevant
  to Apple Macintosh users. To get it, FTP to

  sumex-aim.stanford.edu

  or

  microlib.cc.utexas.edu

  and look for the *mac.ftp.list*. If for some reason you do not find it at
  one of these two sites, run an Archie search with the keyword *mac*.

- *Rover FTP List.* A list of FTP sites, updated every month or so, is
  maintained at the University of Indiana. It is accessible by FTPing
  to *oak.oakland.edu* (a well-known software and file repository).
  Look in pub/msdos/info/ for the ftp-list.zip file.

- *WAIS.* If an Archie search is unsuccessful and you are willing to
  look at potentially unrelated files, try using the WAIS (Wide Area
  Information System) software. WAIS searches the full text of thousands of information resources to find whatever keywords you
  specify. It is an important search tool to master, because it can find
  files in most of the various "areas" of the Internet, whether they
  exist in an FTP site, in a Gopher, on the WWW, in Usenet, or even
  in a Listserv Archive. WAIS is a favorite search tool for many
  people because it allows "natural language queries." Not only can

WAIS search indices and tell you what is there, but it can also retrieve files for you.

WAIS is not without its weaknesses. Although WAIS searches the actual text of files (not just filenames), it does not allow you to specify that keywords must be used together, or in proximity to each other, in a file. In other words, a Boolean-type search which specifies that the words *Internet* and *Marketing* must be used together cannot be done with WAIS. WAIS invariably turns up many files that may use one of your keywords somewhere within its text, but the overall content may have nothing to do with the intent of your search.

It is unlikely that WAIS will evolve into a stronger search mechanism because the consortium of companies that developed it (Thinking Machines, Inc., Apple Computer, and Dow Jones) no longer support the software. Still, if you are willing to cast a wide net in search of information, WAIS can be useful.

WAIS may be running on your local system. If not, try it by telneting to:

quake.think.com

and logging in as *wais*.

- *FTP by E-Mail.* Files accessible by FTP can also be transferred by E-mail if you cannot run FTP for some reason. To do this, you must prepare an E-mail message with the exact sequence of commands you would use if you were actually logged on to an FTP server. The E-mail message is then sent to a special *ftpmail*-server that processes the commands for you. If it is successful in retrieving the file, the ftpmail-server will forward the file to you. Note that the ftpmail-server must specially process the file before it sends the file to you. From three to five commands are used in the process:

connect *address*	(Tells the ftpmail server where the file you want is located)
chdir pub	(Tells the ftpmail server to change to the pub directory)
get filename	(Instructs the ftpmail server to retrieve a file by name)

If the file is binary (and remember, most are), then there are two additional commands to insert before the *get* command:

binary	(Sets file type to binary)
uuencode	(Converts binary file to E-mail-able ASCII text)

The ftpmail-server may take several hours or more to send the file and an accompanying message showing the log of events the server undertook on your behalf.

Telnet

I spoke before about using remote computing resources, such as super computers or library catalogs, through the Internet. These resources are usually available by using the Telnet protocol. Telnet is also referred to as "remote logon" because that is what Telnet makes possible.

BASICS

Telnet is very easy to use, particularly if you use it through a user friendly menu system such as Hytelnet (described later in the section on libraries). Telnet essentially just opens a doorway to another system and then sits back and lets you use the remote system as though you were sitting in front of a terminal at that site (see Figure 7). Like FTP, Telnet requires that you know the exact address of the site you want to visit.

FIGURE 7

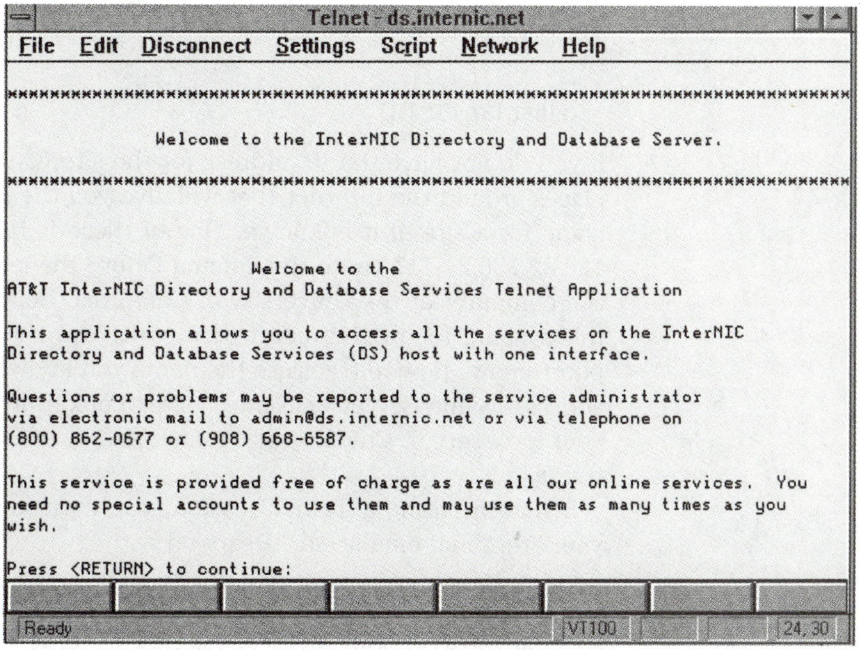

```
┌─────────────────────── Telnet - ds.internic.net ───────────────────────┐
│  File   Edit   Disconnect   Settings   Script   Network   Help          │
├─────────────────────────────────────────────────────────────────────────┤
│ xxxxxxxxxxxxxxxxxxxxxxxxxxxxxxxxxxxxxxxxxxxxxxxxxxxxxxxxxxxxxxxxxxxxxxxxx │
│                                                                         │
│          Welcome to the InterNIC Directory and Database Server.         │
│                                                                         │
│ xxxxxxxxxxxxxxxxxxxxxxxxxxxxxxxxxxxxxxxxxxxxxxxxxxxxxxxxxxxxxxxxxxxxxxxxx │
│                                                                         │
│                                                                         │
│                                                                         │
│                           Welcome to the                                │
│ AT&T InterNIC Directory and Database Services Telnet Application         │
│                                                                         │
│ This application allows you to access all the services on the InterNIC  │
│ Directory and Database Services (DS) host with one interface.           │
│                                                                         │
│ Questions or problems may be reported to the service administrator      │
│ via electronic mail to admin@ds.internic.net or via telephone on        │
│ (800) 862-0677 or (908) 668-6587.                                       │
│                                                                         │
│ This service is provided free of charge as are all our online services. │
│ You need no special accounts to use them and may use them as many times │
│ as you wish.                                                            │
│                                                                         │
│ Press <RETURN> to continue:                                             │
├─────────────────────────────────────────────────────────────────────────┤
│  Ready                                      VT100              24, 30    │
└─────────────────────────────────────────────────────────────────────────┘
```

Once you are logged on to a remote system, you must use the command language and instructions for that specific system. Most of the time, these are UNIX commands (see the section on UNIX commands for more details). If you have problems with these commands, try typing the word *menu* to see if a menu of features for the remote system comes up. Alternately, try the online help at the remote system (just type *help*) and hopefully you will be able to get information on the commands that the remote system recognizes.

Telnet to another system by typing

telnet address

For example, if you wanted to Telnet from your system to mine, you would need to type

telnet ccvax.fullerton.edu

at your system prompt (or fill in this address after launching the Telnet icon in your SLIP/PPP account).

If Telnet fails to connect you, check the address for typing errors and try again. If you still receive an error message, the remote system may be accessible only with its IP (Internet Protocol) address. Every site on the Internet has an IP address, a string of numbers that uniquely identifies each location. If you have a SLIP/PPP connection, your PC has its own IP address, because a SLIP or PPP account elevates the user's machine to a "node" on the Internet. I would Telnet again with the IP address for my university site:

telnet 137.151.1.1

If you do not have the IP address for the site you want, there are a few places around the Internet that will give you the IP equivalent of a text name for a site, if it is known. One of these is reached by telneting to 128.32.136.21,117 (note the comma before the last three digits), which is a computer at the University of California, Berkeley. Once you are in this system, follow the menu prompts to see if the Name Server computer knows how to translate the name you know into the equivalent IP address. Name Server or Name Server Lookup may also be running on your local server. Check your documentation or ask the system administrator.

When initiating a Telnet session, you may sometimes be asked for your "terminal emulation." Respond with

VT-100

Read any instructions given at log on carefully.

Do not forget to properly log off the remote computer when you finish your Telnet session.

Gopher

Because files are stored on computers in a hierarchical structure (organized in *layers* of directories and subdirectories), you may have already realized that it is difficult to browse for information without knowing the exact location of what you want. It can be a lot of work to tunnel down through directories to try to find a particular type of file or filename. A piece of software appropriately called Gopher makes burrowing through files stored on a system much easier, and it even has the built-in capability of retrieving files for you if necessary. The Gopher software makes it look as though each remote computer system is organized in one large database instead of many, many small files. Gopher makes it much less challenging to quickly see what is available at a particular site and then actually look at the contents of a particular file. If the file looks like what you want, Gopher will bring it to you. Gopher can also make the mechanics of jumping from one site to another fairly invisible.

FIGURE 8

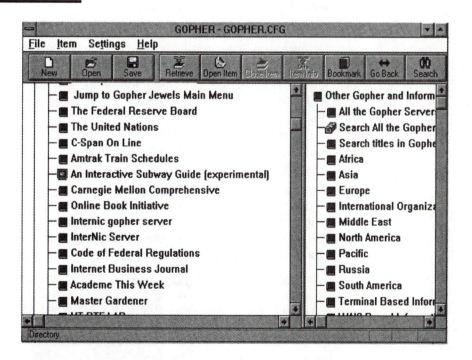

POWER USES

Searching databases is a powerful use of Gopher, particularly when you are looking for just that one fact or statistic to fill in a report. The files are all probably available by either FTP or Telnet, as well, but Gopher provides more informative file descriptions, which helps you narrow down the search quickly. Gopher has some serendipitous properties, too, in that you can browse files using Gopher and may stumble across a treasure trove of information you did not anticipate. Most Gopher menus provide links to other Gopher sites so that you can move between them at will.

Additionally, Gopher provides the capability to "bookmark" favorite locations, so that it is convenient to return to them without having to type in all the address and location information every time.

New Gopher sites are added daily, and they are growing almost as fast as the WWW. In fact, many sites on the WWW are associated with Gopher sites.

Most weaknesses of the Gopher system have to do with the fact that the people who put together the resources available by Gopher develop the naming conventions, and generally those people organizing things are not trained librarians or information professionals but rather system administrators or other computer technical staff. Therefore there is no consistent use of subject headings or keywords, which makes every Gopher different.

BASICS

Gopher client software is probably running on your system, and it can be accessed from within your shell account or by an icon in your SLIP/PPP account. From your shell account system prompt, simply type GOPHER or gopher and the client software should present you with a menu of choices, representing internal information sources and links to external resources.

Use the up or down arrow keys on the keyboard to move to the menu item you want to explore and then press the ENTER key. Items followed by a backslash (/) will present you with another set of menu choices when selected.

After a menu item is selected the system will be busy bringing that information to you. A spinning bar (|) usually appears at the bottom of the screen to let you know the system is working. A typical command summary like the following one is usually visible at the bottom of the screen.

Press ? for help, q to Quit, u to go up a menu Page 2/2

If you find items that you may want to come back to later, leave a *bookmark*. A bookmark will "mark the spot" and in effect create your own personal Gopher menu of favorite resources. Each Gopher client has its own particular bookmark commands, but they all work on the same basic principle.

If you are using a UNIX Gopher client (with a shell account), there are four basic bookmark commands:

a	Adds the item that the arrow key —> is pointing at to your bookmark list.
A	Adds the entire current directory that you are in to your bookmark list.
v	Lets you see the entire bookmark list.
d	Deletes a bookmark from your bookmark list.

It is usually possible to back out of a menu by pressing the ESCAPE (ESC) key or using the quit (q) command.

If you have a SLIP/PPP account, moving around in Gopher is even easier because it can be done by pointing and clicking the mouse, as well as with the arrow keys.

If Gopher software is not available on your system, you can try Gopher by telneting to a public Gopher access site. There are quite a few of these; log in to them with the word *gopher* and the Gopher menu will automatically load. Examples of public sites include:

consultant.micro.umn.edu
gopher.uiuc.edu
gopher.msu.edu

The problem in using Gopher through public access sites is that anything you do in Gopher results in the retrieval of files or resources that require storage space on the system you are logged into as a guest. Use good judgment in using such host systems; do not overload them with files you do not intend to download for use.

End a session by choosing q for Quit. Pressing q twice will usually bring up the command

Really quit? Y/ N

Press Y for Yes and you will be returned to where you started, at your local system prompt or the system prompt at the remote public Gopher access site.

NETIQUETTE

Before sending inflammatory mail to the system administrator, remember that not all Gopher sites are accessible 24 hours a day, 7 days a week. Government and institutional sites may be closed after hours and on weekends, for example. If you receive an error message to the effect that "connection is denied" or "connection could not be made," assume that the system is overloaded or is closed. Naturally, go back and check the address you used, just to make sure there was not a typing error that caused the connection problem.

A basic network etiquette to keep in mind when using Gopher is that although Gopher makes it easy to grab lots of files, storing them on your local system may present a problem for others. There are also copyright and fair use principles to consider when taking copies of remote files.

SEARCH STRATEGIES: VERONICA AND JUGHEAD

It is not necessary to just browse through Gopher menus to find what you want; there are a couple of good search tools to help—Veronica and Jughead (if you are a comic strip fan, you may see where the naming scheme is headed).

Veronica (for Very Easy Rodent Oriented Network Index to Computerized Archives) searches for keywords in any Gopher menu and its associated files and is usually one of the menu options on a Gopher. Periodically Veronica contacts all the known Gophers in the world of connected computers and asks for a copy of its Gopher menus, which Veronica adds to a searchable database. Veronica is similar to Archie, but it improves upon Archie by actually retrieving the file you want, rather than just pointing you to it.

If your local system is not running Veronica, or if it does not appear on the menu of the Gophers you are visiting, try the following server at the University of Minnesota:

gopher.micro.umn.edu 70

Jughead (Jonzie's Universal Gopher Hierarchy Excavation and Display) is more limited than Veronica and a bit harder to access. Jughead restricts searches to Gophers specified by the system administrator. However, in certain cases this can be a benefit, because Veronica can be extremely slow when searching all of gopherspace for a piece of information. Look for Jughead on Gopher menus.

An extensive and regularly updated list of Gopher sites and their contents by subject is Gopher Jewels. A common use of Jughead is searching for keywords on this large master list. You can find Gopher Jewels by doing a Jughead or Veronica search from a Gopher menu.

GOPHER AVAILABLE BY E-MAIL

Just as FTP can be used via E-mail, so can Gopher. It is less convenient than running Gopher client software, but if you are limited to E-mail you can still do research with Gopher, by going through a Gophermail server.

There are four steps to using Gophermail:

1. Prepare an E-mail message addressed to a Gophermail server. Do *not* use the word *help* anywhere in the subject *or* body of the message, unless you want to be sent the Gophermail help

file. Put the keywords of your search argument in the body or subject line instead.

2. Gophermail should respond to your message by sending you its main Gopher menu in the body of an E-mail message. Be patient: The reply may come very quickly or it may take several hours.

3. Reply to the message (using the Reply function in E-mail) and include the text of the message sent to you. Mark on the Gopher menu sent by Gophermail the items you want to see with an X beside them (to the left of the menu item) and send the message back to Gophermail.

4. Gophermail responds to your response by sending the information that you requested. If what you have requested turns out to be another menu, Gophermail sends you the new menu in the body of another E-mail message, and you need to repeat steps 3 and 4 until you get to the actual files you want.

Try Gophermail by sending mail to *gopher@nips.ac.jp* with no message and the word *help* in the subject line. Gophermail will reply with more information on how to use it.

The World Wide Web (WWW)

Just recently considered highly experimental, the World Wide Web (WWW or sometimes W3) is now the fastest growing area of the Internet, thanks to the intense interest of the business community in contributing to its development.

WWW is a simple idea driven by an ambitious agenda: to create a global system of linked and cross-referenced documents contained in computers everywhere. It originated at CERN, the European Laboratory for Particle Physics, as a way for physicists to share their work over the Internet. Similar to Gopher in concept, it differs in several important ways:

- The WWW makes more use of graphics and also has multimedia capabilities (for example, it can carry audio, video, and animation).

- The WWW incorporates Gopher, FTP, Telnet, Usenet news, and some E-mail functions that are helpful in boosting productivity because there is no need to stop working to change to another tool.

"Hypertext" and "hypermedia" are terms associated with the WWW, and they describe the ability of WWW software to create a system of links that permit nearly seamless "branching off" from one document to the next, even if they are on different systems thousands of miles apart. Hypertext links make it easy to follow the trail of an idea from one document or medium to the next and then return to the place you started from (see Figure 9).

FIGURE 9

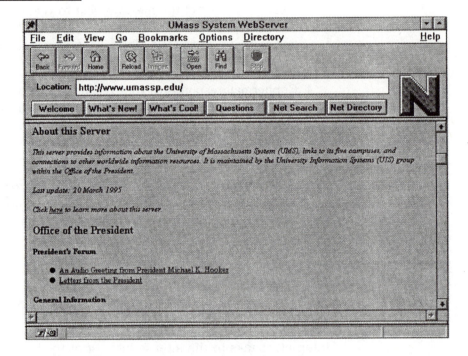

Most experts agree that the future of the Internet is the WWW, and every week more than 1,000 new sites are added to it. It is considered to be a "content-intensive environment," so the materials available through the WWW are a bonanza for the serious researcher of almost any subject.

POWER USES

As I suggested in the preceding paragraphs, one of the most important aspects of the WWW is its "bundling" of several Internet tools in one. Another powerful feature is that the WWW supports "forms," such as fill-in-the-blank surveys or search criteria. This further increases the usefulness of the WWW, because fully interactive searches and market research are possible.

Also, because the business presence on the WWW is growing so rapidly, it is an unparalleled resource for the business student or job seeker, for two reasons:

- Private companies about which detailed information might be difficult or impossible to obtain are adding complete profiles and information about themselves to the WWW, which anyone can see free of cost.

- Employers are looking to the WWW to find employees, often posting available jobs there before advertising in conventional media. Why? Because they want to find employees with good Internet and other technical skills, and going straight to the source makes sense.[10]

Businesses are looking to the WWW as a way of establishing themselves in cyberspace, and many are currently developing secure transaction methods so that it is possible to sell goods and services over the WWW on a large scale. However, despite the millions who visit sites on the WWW daily, it is, oddly enough, considered to be a personalized medium because every user or visitor to a WWW homepage or site in a sense creates his or her own path through the material, depending on what links he or she chooses to follow. Each site is conceivably different for each person visiting it. The WWW is simply a very flexible medium that may very well transform the face of American business.

It is not all business on the WWW. Plenty of sites share recreational pursuits, personal interests, or just wacky achievements like a hottub that is wired to the WWW and can be monitored by anyone tuning in to its WWW site.

BASICS

Individual sites or addresses on the WWW are organized into homepages. In general, the WWW uses a page metaphor to describe its visual interface. Several files or pages may be linked together to make a single homepage (site), and these in turn may link to remote documents or homepages.

WWW sites are accessed with special software called a **browser.** There are a wide variety of browsers to choose from, and each has its particular advantages and disadvantages. The most popular browsers for SLIP/PPP accounts are Mosaic and Netscape. These browsers allow point and click functionality and the ability to see graphics, hear audio, and so on as you are browsing through pages.

Shell accounts on UNIX systems can also access the WWW, but they run nongraphic software such as LYNX. Browsers developed to run on shell accounts have recently been released, and they can handle some of the WWW graphics. One of these is called Slipknot.

The browser retrieves documents and images from WWW servers and displays them on the user's computer, where the information can be saved, printed, or otherwise manipulated. Most browsers allow bookmarks (like those in Gopher) for favorite sites. These are called *hot lists*.

WWW homepages are written with a special programming language known as **HTML** (for **HyperText Markup Language**). Homepages typically have an extension of .html to identify the fact that they were written with HTML code.

Each browser is slightly different, but most come with good documentation (a discussion of each of the top browsers comes later in this section). All have similar basic functions.

Each has a command line where the address of a site can be entered; the address of a site is expressed as a path statement (like FTP). Every hypertext site begins with

http://path.../filename

For example,

http://emporium.turnpike.net/homepage/home.html

In this example, the *http://* tells us that it is supposed to find a hypertext resource (**HTTP** stands for **HyperText Transport Protocol**) at a server called *emporium.turnpike.net*. Once you are at this server, it should look in the homepage directory for a file called *home.html*, and it should display this file on screen. (Note that if I had wanted the browser to retrieve a file by FTP, I would replace the http:// with ftp:// plus the full path and file names. Similarly, ftp:// can be replaced by gopher:// to initiate a Gopher session through the WWW.)

The full address of a WWW resource is called the **Uniform Resource Locator (URL)**. Note that like UNIX, URLs and the WWW are case sensitive.

- Once the document is loaded, the browser should let us pursue links, save the text in a document to a file, mail the document to someone, print the document, or go back or forward to other documents and/or sites.

- If a file is taking too long to load, most browsers have a "bail out" feature. In Netscape, there is a STOP button at the top of the screen. In Mosaic, clicking with the mouse on the spinning globe stops document loading. Other browsers will stop loading when you press the ESCAPE (ESC) key. Before getting started, check on the right way to abort loading.

Hint: WWW sites and documents move around or disappear frequently, just like other materials on the Internet. Sometimes you will not find what you are looking before because it has moved (and has a new path) or because the file name has changed. One way around this is to begin at the end of the path and backspace to the next / symbol and then press the ENTER key. This usually brings up a listing of files in that directory, which can be scanned to see if any files with similar names still exist there. If so, simply move your cursor down to that file and hit ENTER again. This will cause the document to load so you can see its contents.

Popular browsers, all of which are available as shareware in Internet (FTP) archives, and their individual features include:

- *Netscape*. For many, Netscape Navigator (also nicknamed Mozilla) is the undisputed king of WWW browsers because it packs so much into the package. Netscape has been distributed as freeware to educational institutions and is low-cost shareware for everyone else. Netscape is available in Mac, Windows, and UNIX versions. Its primary advantage over other browsers is its speed: Graphics, used rather liberally in many WWW homepages, take longer to load than text and can take a very long time indeed for all but the highest-speed deluxe Internet connections. Many other browsers force users to wait until everything is loaded, but Netscape allows users to begin reading the text while images are loading. An alternative is to stop the images from loading altogether, a feature of most browsers.

- *Mosaic*. Mosaic is the reason the WWW moved from being an experimental toy to almost a force of nature. Initially developed at the National Center for Supercomputing Applications (NCSA), Mosaic includes a built-in hot list and other nice features, but because it insists on loading graphics first and then text, it can be very slow.

Other browsers for SLIP/PPP users are WinWeb and its cousins MacWeb, Cello, and newer offerings such as Internetworks and Samba. For shell account users, the two most popular options are

- *Slipknot*. Slipknot is designed for Windows 3.1 users who are without SLIP/PPP connections but would like to experience some of the graphics capabilities of the WWW. It will run as a dial-up connection through a shell account. It actually works by launching Lynx from your local server and then adding images. Links and documents can be bookmarked, and Slipknot has the advantage of allowing you to save text as well as images from your favorite sites to your hard drive.

- *Lynx*. Lynx is an easy-to-use UNIX WWW browser. Before Slipknot it was the only solution for those without a SLIP/PPP connection. It does not display graphics or multimedia but is an extremely efficient text browser. I often use the Lynx client software when I am looking for something specific and do not wish to be slowed down by graphics or other distractions.

If Lynx is not running on your local server, you can try it out by telneting to

ukanaix.cc.ukans.edu (log in as www)

To use a browser, you need to start out with an initial WWW site address so that you can follow links to other sites. Good places to begin are some of the subject-oriented directories discussed in the next section.

SEARCH STRATEGIES

A comparatively large number of search engines and subject-oriented directories have sprung up to help WWW users find resources. The problem with the search engines is that each one searches for topics in its own way. Similarly, each subject directory organizes resources in its own way. Because there is no "top level" to the WWW, because there is no real central authority, and because millions of resources scattered all around the globe are attached to it, the WWW can be very confusing at first. Aimless browsing can be amusing for a short time because you can run into fascinating and even bizarre information, but it can never be productive over the long run. The best thing prospective WWW users can do is learn about the various search engines and directories and their associated strengths and weaknesses so that it becomes clear when it is appropriate to use one tool and when to use another.

The search engines differ significantly in their methods of data collection. One distinction is that some engines go out to known WWW sites and gather information about the content of materials there (*spider-based searching*) and some wait for others to add pointers to it (*directory-based searching*). It is usually wise to try out your keywords with several search engines during any one search.

Good subject-oriented directories can be found at Yahoo, the Virtual Library, EINet Galaxy, the Planet Earth Page, and GNN Whole Internet Catalog.

- *Yahoo.* Yahoo is a directory service launched by two Stanford University students, and it has recently spun off from the university as a commercial service. Searching it is currently free to users. Yahoo supports keyword searches. The "What's New" page, updated almost daily, is must reading for many people each morning. You can find it at

  http://www.yahoo.com

- *The Virtual Library.* The library includes a huge list of sites maintained at CERN, the father of the WWW. Contact

  http://info.cern.ch/hypertext/DataSources/bySubject/Overview.html

- *EINet Galaxy.* This directory supports keyword searches and also allows searches of other directories from this site. It is organized somewhat like the Virtual Library. Contact

  http://www.einet.net

- *The Planet Earth Page.* This is an easy-to-use, graphically oriented catalog. Beware: All those graphics can take a long time to load; you may need to abort. Contact

  http://white.nosc.mil/info_modern.html

- *GNN Whole Internet Catalog*   This catalog is well organized but not comprehensive. Contact

  http://nearnet.gnn.com/wic/newrescat.toc.html

Spider-based search engines send out automated bits of code (also known as robots, bots, and worms) to search known WWW sites for content. These search engines differ because some take a *depth-first approach* and others a *breadth-first approach.* Depth searches are done by starting with a particular document and following every link in it, one after another, logging the content, then going on to the next document. Depth searches sound like an ideal and thorough way to catalog the Internet, but with the explosive growth of WWW resources, they simply take too long and slow down systems too much to be reasonable. Breadth searches do not follow each link to its exhaustive conclusion. Rather, this type of search focuses on top-level WWW homepages and describes their contents.

Besides depth-versus-breadth searching, spider-based search engines differ in the way they make "decisions" about the relative weight of descriptors, whether or not Boolean searching is permitted, and so on.

Currently the WWW is undergoing a transition, and many resources that were previously free of charge are becoming commercial services. New fee-based services, such as the InfoSeek service, a high-quality spider-based search engine, offer improvements. It is believed that as more commercial services are added, there will be stronger incentives to develop comprehensive search mechanisms. Until then, however, the following are the most popular spider-based search tools.

- *Lycos.* Lycos makes a "weighted choice" about which documents to report back to you upon executing a search, preferring to choose documents that have shorter URLs (paths) and those with multiple links (from other sites or documents) pointing to them. The rationale for this is that shorter paths are shallower and therefore have more breadth (Lycos is a breadth-searcher). Document popularity, signaled by the number of "crosslists" Lycos senses, is also a factor, and it is interpreted as a kind of validation index.[11] Use Lycos at

http://lycos.cs.cmu.edu

- *The WWW Worm (WWWW)*. Using the WWWW is easier if you know the key UNIX commands, and WWWW is able to perform searches, not just for keywords in page contents or titles. It also looks at the URL, file name, address, and other factors. Use the WWWW at

http://www.cs.colorado.edu/home/mcbryan/WWWW.html

- *Webcrawler*. Webcrawler tries to marry depth and breadth searching (and occasionally succeeds) but is notable because it allows proximity and Boolean searches, plus it indexes content as well as titles of pages. Try Webcrawler at

http://www.biotech.washington.edu/WebCrawler/Home.html

- *Jumpstation II*. Jumpstation II is broad based but cannot search for both title and document keywords simultaneously. Try Jumpstation at

http://www.stir.ac.uk/jsbin/jsii

A collection of search engines, all on one page, can be found at

http://cuiwww-unige.ch/meta-index.html

PUBLISHING YOUR OWN HOMEPAGE

Some schools and universities offer students and faculty a chance to become WWW "publishers" by providing WWW server space for personal homepages. Faculty are using WWW homepages to share their research findings, provide a central location for class materials and syllabi, and as a repository for other information. Student homepages have been known to cover everything from favorite downtown bars, complete with photographs, to papers on nucleic acid sequences.

Homepages with graphics, forms, and other special features can be elaborate and require expert design services. Still, if you are fortunate enough to get free or low cost space for your own homepage, do not be intimidated by the thought of writing simple HTML code. Only a few

HTML commands are necessary, and they are quite straightforward. With the aid of an ASCII text editor or any one of several HTML packages (such as HTML Assistant, available as shareware on the Internet), you can create a basic, attractive homepage in a few minutes. Also, HTML converters have been released as add-ons for registered users of Microsoft Word or WordPerfect, and these programs make producing a simple homepage even easier.

Your system administrator may have a handout on writing basic HTML code. If not, look for instruction manuals such as Lemay's *Teach Yourself Web Publishing with HTML.* Avoid the beginner's sin of using too many inline images (graphics) on your page, though, because they irritate others who have to wait a long time for the graphics to load.

Once you have a homepage, you should "register" it in several places so that people can find you. Do this by going to one or more of the major directories (listed earlier) and looking for the ADD command. The directory will need the complete http:// path and filename information, information about how to contact you, and a brief description of the contents of the page.

WWW AVAILABLE BY E-MAIL

If WWW access is not available through your current account but you know what documents or sites you wish to visit, you can retrieve WWW homepages through your E-mail account. However, it is a tricky procedure, and a procedure which is still evolving. If you would like updated information on how to do this, send E-mail to one or both of the following:

listserv@info.cern.ch
(blank subject line; type only *www* in the body of the message)
webmail@curia.ucc.ie
(blank subject line; type only *help* in the body of the message)

WWW AVAILABLE BY FAX

Failing all else, you can now retrieve WWW homepages by fax from a company called Universal Access in Santa Barbara, California. If you use a touch-tone telephone, the URL is translated to a numeric ID, the document and any images are retrieved, and it is all sent to any fax machine you specify. Audio files attached to documents can be played for the user over the telephone. This service, announced in April of 1995, is currently free in its introductory phase but will be fee-based in the future. Send E-mail for information to

info@ua.com

Now that you are familiar with the most important Internet tools, let's talk a little more about what you can do with them.

Applying the Tools

ONLINE LIBRARIES: WHAT LIBRARIES HAVE TO OFFER

Some of the best features of the Internet are the thousands of library catalogs and online databases made publicly available by universities, colleges, and governments around the world. Although very few have digitized their collections (so few full-text books are available), most have comprehensive electronic catalogs that can be searched, saving the researcher considerable time in locating unusual or out-of-print titles, journals, and other materials. Because the Library of Congress receives a copy of every book published in the United States (as well as many published in other countries), it is frequently used as a substitute for the *Books in Print* directories, which are commercial products and not yet available online. Online libraries also commonly have pointers to other resources or searchable subject-area databases.

Locating Online Library Resources   Most libraries are accessible only by Telnet, an Internet tool that allows you to run programs or search databases on a remote computer from your own keyboard, or Gopher, a browsing tool that can also locally retrieve documents. Telnet requires that you know the exact "address" of the library you want to "visit" (more on Telnet soon), and it does not let you download a document directly. The Gopher software is preferable to Telnet. Some libraries, however, are building programs so that their databases can be searched through the World Wide Web (WWW) interface, which is a simplified, hypertext-based interface. Many pointers to library catalogs exist around the Internet, and there are also pointers to some of the better-known collections in the appendix of this book .

For a comprehensive catalog of Internet-accessible libraries, visit a server running the Hytelnet software, which is basically a regularly updated list of online resources available by Telnet with an easy-to-use menu. When you choose a resource with Hytelnet, it will either connect you to that resource automatically or show you how to access it. You can try Hytelnet at

telnet access.usask.ca

or

telnet info.ccit.arizona.edu

If you are running a SLIP/PPP connection, you can download Hytelnet software and run it on your own PC. To find it, run an Archie search with Hytelnet as the keyword.

You can also try the Launchpad or Eureka services. Launchpad, located at the University of North Carolina, performs searches and allows you to access many library systems. Eureka, based at Stanford University, is also an easy-to-use search service, but it has the added advantage of providing access to the vast online resources of the Research Libraries Group (RLG) and the Research Libraries Information Network (RLIN) bibliographic files. Eureka is a gateway to more than 25 million books, journals, archives, and other materials. You can find them at

Launchpad: telnet: launchpad.unc.edu (log in: *launch)*
Eureka: Telnet: eureka-info.stanford.edu

Another resource you will want to visit is Project Gutenberg's archive of digitized full-text classic books, where *Moby Dick* and *Pride and Prejudice* and dozens of other texts can be found and downloaded. This can be a lifesaver if you are doing detailed content analyses or if every bookstore and library in your small town are out of a book after its adaptation comes out in movie theaters. Project Gutenberg texts are mirrored (copied to other servers) throughout the Internet; however, you should be able to find them by Telnet at

nysernet.org (log in: nysernet)

or do a WAIS or Archie search.

Becoming Your Own Reference Librarian   In the absence of your own personal online reference librarian (or at least a "smart agent" that "thinks" like one), you need to learn a set of flexible search strategies to maximize your use of time. Internet-wide search tools like WAIS, Archie, Veronica, and Lycos are important, but flexibility and patience are just as critical.

One thing to keep in mind is that search- and menu-driven commands at each local library site can differ, and online documentation is sometimes missing or not available. Furthermore, log-on and log-off procedures can also be different from system to system. It will not always be clear what the computer expects, so it is important to try different approaches and, when you enter a system, watch for any prompts that will tell you how to log in properly and navigate that local system.

Online searching is mostly based on Boolean algebra, which "broadens and narrows sets using the operators AND, OR and NOT." Boolean searching can be very efficient, but only if you have refined your concepts and developed an appropriate strategy first.

For example, you are interested in doing research on women in television. You want to know about their roles, statistics on how many women are involved in all aspects of television production, and the historical evolution of women in the industry.

1. Your research question is broken down into specific concepts. (I did this in the preceding paragraph. Let me say once again that this step is an extremely important part of the process, because failure to recognize that there are multiple and distinct concepts or terms embedded in your research question will produce unsatisfactory and incomplete search results.)

2. The concepts are expressed as

   a. Keywords: A few words that describe the essential concepts. (You can start out with the keywords *women*, *television*, and *history*.)

   b. Synonyms: Are there synonyms that you could use instead of the keywords? If so, include them in the keywords. (In this case, *history* could be synonymous with *evolution*, as in "Women and the Evolution of Television." Conceivably an article or book could have been written with this alternative title or subject heading.)

3. A "search set" is built using this information.

   Set 1. women

   Set 2. television

   Set 3. history or evolution

4. Boolean connections are made between the sets

   Set 1 AND Set 2 AND Set 3

   women AND television AND history OR evolution

5. Running the search should produce only citations that are relevant to the research question. However, errors in set construction can produce unrelated materials. For example, if you expressed the Boolean set as *women* AND *television* OR *history* OR *evolution*, you would probably receive a large number of citations on the Darwinian theories of evolution, anything with the word history in its title, and possibly, buried among them all, a few pertinent citations on the topic of women and television (but not their historical role in it).

Some librarians are available to answer occasional questions on the Internet—some for a nominal fee and some free of charge—if the subject is one in which they feel they have specific knowledge.

Librarians both subscribe to and moderate Listservs on many different topics, and if your questions are well thought out and politely phrased, you may be able to get online help from a professional librarian. However, this is no substitute for learning the basic search methods yourself, because librarians are busy people who naturally see their primary responsibilities as belonging to their own institutions or organizations.

Online Databases   Thousands, perhaps millions, of databases are currently online, ranging from song lyrics to the U.S. Census. The Internet permits direct access to the data and the ability to manipulate them, often extending to downloading them to your own PC software or workstation. All kinds of data are available, so doing secondary analysis of raw data is much easier than it once was. In addition, once you have located the data you want, the Internet has statistical software that you can use to analyze it.

Use WAIS, Archie, or one of the WWW search engines (all discussed later in this section) to find a database with a keyword search. Some of the databases you may find useful include:

- ERIC (Educational Resources Information Center). Locate several sites with WAIS.

- ICPSR (Inter-University Consortium of Political and Social Research). Start by visiting the ICPSR Gopher at

  gopher.icpsr.umich.edu

- United States Geological Survey (USGS) (fault maps, GIS information, seismological research, and more). Locate it at

  Gopher: **oemg.er.usgs.gov**

- National Space Science Data Center (NSSDC) (astrophysics, earth sciences, space physics, planetary sciences, etc.). Locate it at

  telnet: **nssdca.gsfc.nas.gov** (log in as nodis)

- NASA Lunar and Planetary Institute. Locate it at

  telnet: **lpi.jsc.nasa.gov** (log in as lpi)

- GenBank Database (nucleic acids sequences). Locate it at

  Gopher: **ftp.bio.indiana.edu**

An Important Note: Although I have provided the addresses of some notable resources, do *not* rely on published "addresses" of resources, because on the Internet they change fairly often. Changes occur because an organization adds a new computer and moves resources to another server or because sponsorship of the resource is moved. For example, in 1994 many resources were moved from Gopher sites to the WWW. Once it became clear how popular and user-friendly the WWW was, it made sense to move them. The next generation of tools may make every address in this book and others obsolete, but as long as you know how to perform well-planned searches and have good research skills, you will always be able to find many of the resources and data you need.

Remote Computing Features   Occasionally you may need to use computing resources, such as supercomputers, that are beyond those available to you locally. The Internet offers access to a wide array of remote computing resources, although access usually involves applying for accounts or other access permissions. If you find a resource that requires anything other than "anonymous" or "guest" log-in names, you have reached a private server that you must have permission to enter and use. Avoid use of remote resources that can disrupt or slow traffic at that site. For example, it is considered extremely poor network etiquette to store on remote systems files that you should be storing on your own personal or network computer, because systems slow down proportionate to the available space, memory, and traffic.

Online Communications

The Internet offers two basic kinds of communications with other people: (1) electronic mail based systems (Usenet News, Listservs, and various electronic mail programs) that are asynchronous, and (2) interactive real-time communications using protocols such as Internet Relay Chat or one of the multi-user domains.

ELECTRONIC MAIL: HOW E-MAIL AND DISCUSSION GROUPS CAN BE POWER RESEARCH TOOLS

Electronic mail (E-mail) is indeed a power research tool if for no other reason than it reaches so many people, some of whom—such as celebrities, senior executives, and experts—are not easily accessible in other ways. Even if all you have is an E-mail account, the entire Internet is available with just a little extra effort. Any WWW page can be sent to you by E-mail if you do not have a browser. Usenet posts can be sent via E-mail, and even software and other files can be attached to E-mail messages.

Power Uses: Finding Experts, Interviewing, Information Retrieval, etc. Using the Internet to enhance your productivity usually means you need one of the following functions:

1. You need to find *experts* or authorities in a particular subject area for interviews or references/referrals.

2. You need to *interview* nonexperts or authorities concerning a particular subject area or monitor discussions on a particular topic.

3. You need to find *data* or *tools*, such as subject information, statistics, software, documents, or files.

Businesses are now using the Internet to market products and services, so *advertising* and *promotion* are also functions that the Internet facilitates. However, businesses promote themselves within the Internet's content-intensive environment, so the provision of information or "content" is intrinsically related to Internet marketing. Many commercial sites hold data or information that could be important for you. Therefore, from the researcher's point of view, this function is best placed under the category of finding data or tools.

No one Internet tool allows you to perform all these functions, although new World Wide Web browsing software, such as Netscape, comes very close. Thus it is important to learn the most efficient and productive techniques for using each of several tools, such as electronic mail, Telnet, FTP, Gopher, the WWW, WAIS, and Archie. The rest of this chapter is devoted to a discussion of the various Internet tools and how to use them.

MORE ON INTERNET CULTURE

Many newcomers to the Internet (newbies) are surprised to find how friendly Internet old-timers are, how approachable they are, and how willing they are to help smooth the snags of the learning curve. With the Internet growing at around 15% to 20% a month, however, the fabled courtesies of network users may change as they are subjected to an onslaught of newbies who do not know about or do not respect the unique user culture. For the most part, the culture of the Internet is a research-oriented one, because long-time users have been mostly scientists and academicians.[12] The research culture expects a certain level of technical competence and a willingness to mutually engage in a free exchange of information. "Technical competence" means that new users should take the time to learn about basic Internet tools (as you are doing by reading this book) and should avoid wasting other people's online time by asking trivial questions (How do I send an E-mail message?) that can be easily answered by any basic textbook. If you want to benefit from the knowledge and expertise of others on the Net, you *must* be sensitive to netiquette and acceptable use guidelines, just as you would be if you were visiting a foreign country. On the Internet, when the press of a button can take you from Japan to Bolivia, you really are a foreign traveler. Be cautious about asking for help, pointers, or other favors until you understand the climate of the Internet and the specific area of it in which you are engaged.

The Internet Treasure Hunt: Learning with the Net

An enterprising Internet citizen, Rick Gates, wanted to test his and others' knowledge of the Internet and its informational resources, so in September of 1992 he announced "The Internet Hunt." For each Hunt, Gates posted a research question in various places around the Net and invited others to try to find the answer. Answers had to come directly from Internet resources, and the entrants had to explain how they found the answer. In this way Gates shared information about the wide variety of Internet resources that were popping up every day and helped nurture creative research strategies for finding and using information.

The Hunt is still going on, although the number of competitors in each Hunt has increased from the original handful. Reading the Hunt archives, and eventually participating in the Hunt competitions, can greatly increase your knowledge of Internet resources and the research process.

You can see the archives of the Hunt at:

gopher.cic.net

or

ftp.cic.net/pub/hunt

or on the WWW at

http://www.hunt.org/

Happy hunting!

RFCs: Getting More Technical Information

If you are interested in the inner workings of Internet policy-making bodies or the technical details of the Internet **backbone**, standards, or protocols, you can find a large amount of information in the form of **requests for comments (RFCs)**. RFCs are created by research and technical communities and are publicly available.

An RFC, once accepted, is assigned a number and kept online in an archive. RFCs can be retrieved by FTP at

ds.internic.net/rfc

Unless you know the exact number of the RFC you want, you need to retrieve the index first and then go back and copy the files you want.

Entertainment and the Internet: Games and MUDs

Because the overall purpose of this book is to show how the Internet can be used for research and other productive work, I have not emphasized the recreational opportunities available on the Internet. The Internet is indeed a rich and varied landscape for leisure, and it has thousands of games; chat forums; and interactive, alternative "spaces," such as Multi-User Domains (MUDs). MUDs are largely experimental, with great potential as virtual workplaces and learning environments, but for now they are mostly for interactive gaming. MUDs are constantly being formed and disbanded, but if you have some time to spare they are fascinating places to visit. I recommend reading the available MUD FAQs (do an Archie or a WAIS search to find them) and picking up one of the specialized books on Internet games and adventures, such as Michael Wolff's *Netgames: Your Guide to the Games People Play on the Electronic Highway* (Random House)[13] or Eddy's *Internet After Hours* (Prima).[14]

Notes on Configuring TCP Manager and Windows 3.1 for a SLIP/PPP Connection

If you are fortunate enough to have access to a SLIP/PPP Internet connection, you were probably given software that enables you to set up and make the appropriate connection to the university or other server. Occasionally a technical support person will help you do this, but more often you are asked to do your own installation.

Setting up a SLIP/PPP connection requires that you have several pieces of information from your computing center about your account, and that you configure the software accordingly. Most of this software is what is known as *shareware*, which is software that is supplied free of charge for a trial period, but you are required to pay for it if you decide to continue using it.

Following are a few notes relevant to setting up the Trumpet TCP Manager (TCPMAN) software within Windows 3.1. If you plan to run TCP Manager on a Macintosh, the software is similar but the initial configuration is somewhat different. Ask technical support or a friend to help install TCP Manager on a Mac. Other software similar to TCP Manager is available as shareware, but the Trumpet TCP Manager is the one most commonly used.

The TCP Manager software is used at the start of an Internet session, and its only function is to establish and maintain the connection between your computer and the Internet. Once the connection is established, the TCP Manager software "sits in the background" until you finish the session, and then you return to the TCP Manager program and ask it to disconnect the session.

Windows 95 includes a TCP/IP stack. To configure Windows 95 for an Internet connection, follow the instructions in Microsoft's Windows Internet Setup Wizard. Installing the Microsoft Network (MSN) has led to some problems with existing communications packages that may be on your system. Microsoft has announced that it will correct these problems soon.

Initial Software Installation

Most software packages supplied by access providers come to you "compressed." That is, the files have been compressed using a special program to save space and improve portability. The standard compression software is called PKZIP and PKUNZIP and is widely available. Windows 3.1 and PC Tools File Manager should offer an EXPAND command that allows you to "unzip" compressed files with a .zip extension (as in "myfile.zip"). Copy the compressed files into a new, empty directory and from file manager in Windows 3.1 click on the filename and EXPAND. After the file is uncompressed, you will probably have several files. These may need to be further set up in Windows by using the RUN command and "install.exe" or "setup.exe" files. Continue until you are set up successfully and all your Internet applications are grouped together in a program.

CHECKING WINDOWS' CONFIGURATION

Turn on your computer and start Windows. Open the Main icon group and click on Control Panel (see Figure 10). It may take a few moments for the control panel to load all its drivers.

FIGURE 10

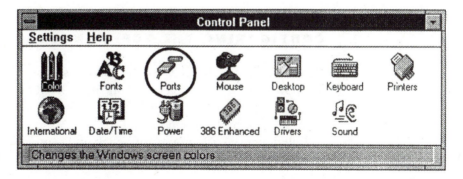

Next click on Ports and select the port your modem is on (see Figure 11).

FIGURE 11

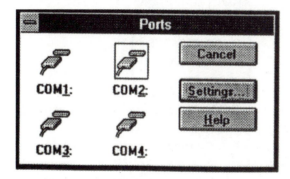

Enter the modem speed setting (19200 will work for a 14400 modem, but choose a lower speed for slower modems and a higher speed only if you have a 28.8K v.34 modem) and match the rest of the settings in Figure 12.

FIGURE 12

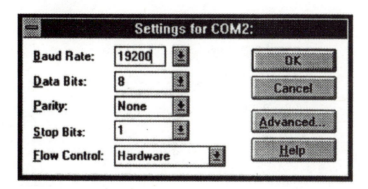

After you have done this, click OK and then close the Ports box, the Control Panel, and the Main Group.

CONFIGURING THE TCP MANAGER

When the TCP Manager is installed, its icon will appear on your Windows desktop. Double-click on the TCP Manager icon to load the program. Now you must configure it with the specific information for your account and connection.

Pull down the File menu, and click on Setup (see Figure 13).

FIGURE   13

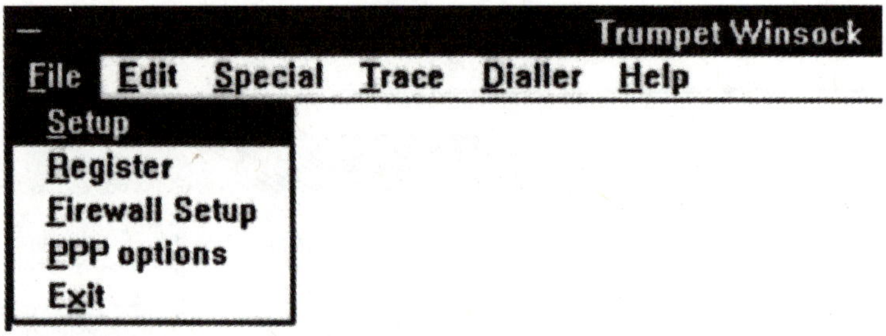

The network configuration box appears. The network configuration box is where you must enter key information about your account and the location of the server to which you will be connected. You will not be able to determine this by trial and error or by any method other than asking your account provider to give you the exact numbers and data. Use the following worksheet to fill in the information. The information that you need includes:

IP address: _____

Net mask: _____

Name server: _____

Default gateway: _____

Domain server: _____

Domain suffix: _____

SLIP port: _____
(The port number your modem is connected to is either 1, 2, 3, or 4.)

Baud rate: _____
(The speed of your modem)

Later you can try to set this higher for faster performance, but for now choose the rated speed of your modem.

After making changes in the settings click on OK and then close the Trumpet TCP Manager (that is, go back to Program Manager). Start the Trumpet TCP Manager again to allow the changes to take effect.

Once you are happy with the settings in the TCP Manager, pull down the Dialler menu and select 1 setup.cmd (see Figure 14).

FIGURE 14

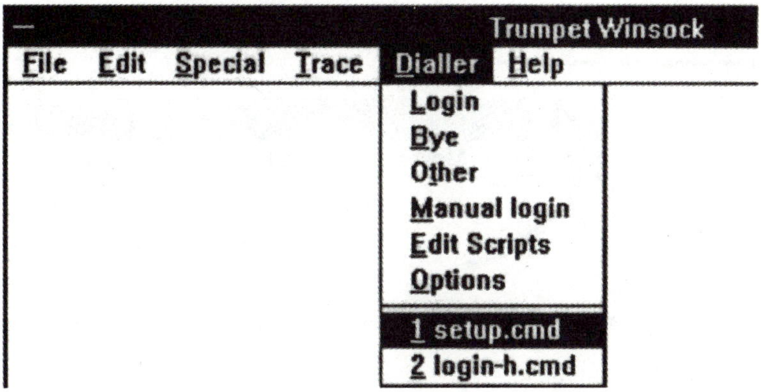

You will be asked to enter the dial-in phone number to which you will be connecting, your account user name (that is, your ID), and your password. SLIP/PPP user names and passwords are different from those you might have been assigned with a regular or shell account.

When you have entered your ID and your password, you should then be able to connect to the Internet by pulling down the Dialler menu and clicking on Login. There may be a screeching sound for a few seconds, somewhat like the tone for a fax machine, and some text will scroll across the screen as your connection to the Internet is established. This should last from 10 to 15 seconds.

The process is complete when your IP address shows up at the bottom of the screen, and you may also get a message saying "you are connected" or "SLIP ENABLED." *If the address doesn't appear, then you are not connected to the Internet, and none of the rest of your Internet software will work.* For some accounts, the IP address is dynamic, which means that this address will change from one session to the next because it is temporary, valid only while you are connected to the Internet. Other accounts have a permanent IP address that will always appear when you connect.

Once the connection has been established, click on the down arrow in the upper right-hand corner of the window to *minimize* it. The

Trumpet TCP Manager will run in the background for the duration of your Internet session, assisting the rest of your Internet software as it communicates with various Internet sites.

ENDING THE SESSION/DISCONNECTING

Part One: Locating the Trumpet TCP Manager   When the time comes to wrap up the Internet session, the first thing to do is to find the Trumpet TCP Manager window. This can be accomplished by pulling down the Window Control menu in any Windows application (see Figure 15).

FIGURE   15

Select Switch To . . . from the Window Control menu (see Figure 16).

FIGURE   16

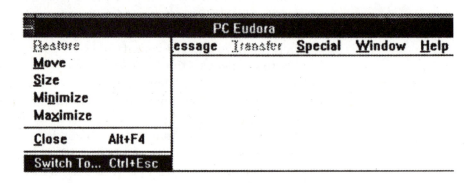

The Task List will appear, and you can select Trumpet TCP Manager from it. Highlight Trumpet TCP Manager, then click on Switch To. The Trumpet TCP Manager window will reappear. Now you can disconnect.

Part Two: Disconnecting   To disconnect from the Internet properly, you must pull down the Dialler menu and select Bye. You should get a PPP DISABLED or SLIP DISABLED message at the bottom of the screen.

In a real session it is now time to close down any other Internet software that is still operating. After that, you can exit from the Trumpet TCP Manager by pulling down the File menu and selecting Exit (see Figure 17). You should now be off line.

FIGURE 17

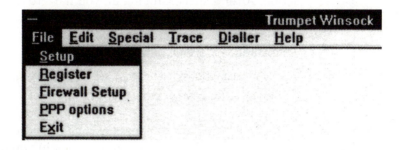

Troubleshooting

LOGGING IN

When you are trying to log in and you get a "modem not responding" message, there is a conflict in your serial port settings or your IRQ settings. Check

1. The Trumpet TCP Manager software setup.

2. The modem dip switches or jumper settings (especially if it's a new installation).

3. The setup of other peripherals (sound card, printers, etc.) for IRQ conflicts.

NO IP ADDRESS

When the log-in procedure is finished, the last lines on your screen should look like the following:

Trumpet TCP Manager negotiating PPP Connection

Script completed
PPP ENABLED
My IP address = 189.182.3.3

The IP address will be different, but *if you don't get this line, you are not properly logged in* and you will have trouble getting things to work. The most common cause is that the Trumpet TCP Manager File/Setup box is not filled out properly. If you haven't connected yet, check your comm settings (modem and Windows) and your IRQ settings.

TWO IMPORTANT POINTS

1. Your Internet server will log you off if you don't take immediate action. After a successful log in, you have to do something right away. If you wait too long (more than a minute or so), many servers quietly disconnect you without notification. After that, everything you try will fail.

2. You cannot log back in immediately after using the Bye command. You may decide to log off the network and work off line for a while. If you use the Bye command from the Dialler menu in Trumpet TCP Manager, your IP address is not flushed from the setup field. When you log back in you do not usually get a new address, and nothing will work.

If you use the Bye command, you must do *one of two things* before logging back in:

1. Use File/Setup to open the network configuration box and reset the IP address field to 0.0.0.0 (type a zero and then press enter twice).

2. Exit from the Trumpet TCP Manager and then start it again.

If you go off line in the middle of a session (intentionally or otherwise), before reconnecting you must shut down all your Internet software and start again with the Trumpet TCP Manager.

Occasionally you will get inexplicable results, particularly if you have experienced trouble in an application and received a "general protection fault" message from Windows. The best thing to do is to quit all your Internet software, log off, exit back to Windows' program manager, and start over. Occasionally you may have to quit Windows completely and restart it to get everything working properly again.

Remember that this book and other Internet guides will be invaluable in helping you to avoid some of the frustrations of being online. However, it is absolutely inevitable that sooner or later you will come face to face with puzzling results no matter how carefully you follow instructions. Often, failure to connect to a resource or turn up an expected search result are due to problems with the network (maybe a server in the path is down, out of service, being repaired, etc.) or with the computer to which you are trying to connect. It is equally likely, though, that you have made an error in typing a command, address, or some other aspect of the procedure that is causing problems.

Computers are intolerant of things like spelling errors, and they are without "artificial intelligence" capabilities and cannot make the kinds of simple connections between concepts that human beings do. Be patient, stay calm, and do not worry if the result you expect does not turn up immediately. Try to become flexible in your approach and troubleshoot problems as they crop up. This method will provide further insights into the way computers and networks operate, and in a short time you will not be perplexed by the usual online obstacles.

Endnotes

1. Lohr, S. (1994). Status @sym.bol on the 'Net.'

2. Jacobs, D. (1995, January 3). Businesses Admit Snooping on Workers. *The San Diego Union-Tribune*, p. C4.

3. Cybercriminals Beware! (1994, October). *Medea Magazine,* p. 36.

4. Angell, D., & Heslop, B. (1994). *The Elements of E-Mail Style: Communicate Effectively via Electronic Mail.* Addison-Wesley Publishing Company.

5. Warren, D. (1994, October). Is It Love or Is It Cybersex? *Newmedia,* p. 127.

6. Kushner, D. (1994, December). DragNet: Confessions of a Cyberlesbian. *Details,* p. 76.

7. We, G. (1994, July 26). Cross Gender Communication in Cyberspace. *Electronic Journal of Virtual Culture.* (ftp://byrd.mu.wvnet.edu/pub/ejvc/we.v2n3)

8. Truong, H. (1993, March). Gender Issues in Online Communications. In *3rd Annual Conference, Computers, Freedom and Privacy.* San Francisco.

9. Rapp, A. (1994, October). Virtual Therapy. *Newmedia,* p. 127.

10. Soreff, Z. (1995, April). Our Brilliant Careers. *Netguide,* pp. 49–56.

11. Weiss, A. (1995, April). Hop Skip and Jump. *Internet World,* p. 41.

12. Waldrop, M. M. (1994, August 12). Culture Shock on the Networks. *Science,* pp. 879–881.

13. Wolff, M. (1994). *Netgames: Your Guide to the Games People Play on the Electronic Highway.* Random House.

14. Eddy, A. (1994). *Internet After Hours.* Prima.

4

The Ever-Mutating Net: Keeping Up with Changes

In the last sections we examined some of the implications of the Internet for research, as well as how to use the most important Internet tools. Before that, however, I discussed the explosive growth of the Internet over the past several years. This continued pattern of growth makes keeping up with the Internet very difficult, yet anyone who plans to use it for work and scholarship must also make a commitment to keep abreast of changes. The Internet Treasure Hunt, discussed in Part 3, will keep your research skills sharp. But how do you keep up with other things that are happening on the Net? In fact, there are a number of ways to keep in touch with new online resources and opportunities; we look at several of them in this section.

Online Resources

Descriptions of and addresses for some of the most helpful online resources for keeping up with the changes follow.

INTERNIC

The InterNIC is a cooperative project among several organizations, and it is concerned with providing information about Internet access, resources, and registering new networks. NIC stands for Network Information Center. Established in 1993 by the National Science Foundation, it is also supported by General Atomics, AT&T, and Network Solutions, Inc. InterNIC makes available a mammoth reference catalog of Internet resources and sites (the *Directory of Directories*) as well as information about new domains, and it also publishes a number of newsletters on various topics. Because new networks and domains must register with InterNIC, it is an excellent source for information on trends. In addition, the *Directory of Directories* is a good place to begin looking for information on a particular topic or company.

To find the *Directory of Directories*, you can use the following addresses:

Telnet: **ds.internic.net** (log in as guest or new user to get an introductory tutorial)
gopher: **gopher.internic.net** (log in as gopher)

On the WWW, enter

http://ds.internic.net/ds/dsdirofdirs.html

For InterNIC Reference Desk and Education Services, enter

telnet: **is.internic.net (log in anonymous)**

Also, see the Scout Report.

The Scout Report   The Scout Report, a weekly publication by InterNIC's Information Services division, provides highlights of new and noteworthy online resources for the week. It can be accessed via Gopher, the WWW, or sent automatically to you by E-mail every week. It is written primarily for the research and academic communities so it is relevant to your interests. To access the Scout Report as E-mail,

- Send a message to

    majordomo@is.internic.net

- Leave the subject blank or insert a blank space if necessary.

- In the body of the message, type

    subscribe scout-report

- Send the message.

You should receive a confirmation message and a Scout Report by E-mail once a week until you unsubscribe from the list.

On the WWW, go to

http://www.internic.net/infoguide.html

By Gopher, type

is.internic.net

Once you are connected to the InterNIC Gopher, select Information Services/Scout Report to read the text.

Net-Happenings List   Another InterNIC service, the Net-Happenings list, sends subscribers daily digests on new online resources and events of note, such as conference announcements, publications, calls for papers, and tools. It is moderated and is compiled from a surprisingly broad range of sources. To access Net-Happenings archives, follow these steps.

- To see the archives of current and previous digests, send E-mail to

    majordomo@is.internic.net

- Leave the subject blank; in message body type

    index net-happenings-digest

- Send the message.

These steps should result in a return message that lists back issues of Net-Happenings by topics.

To retrieve any digest by E-mail,

- Send E-mail to

    majordomo@is.internic.net

- Leave subject blank; in message body type

    get net-happenings-digest v/n

- Replace v/n in the preceding line with the volume and number of the digest you want to retrieve.

The Net-Happenings List recently became available as a Usenet newsgroup under the name *comp.internet.net-happenings*.

WWW "WHAT'S NEW" SERVICES

Because the WWW is experiencing the largest growth of all Internet services at the same time that it is becoming synonymous with a popular understanding of what the Internet is, it is just about certain that the WWW will have the lion's share of new sites and services. In mid-1995 there were roughly 400 to 500 new WWW sites reported every day, and most experts are predicting that number will at least double within a year. Clearly no single person can visit 500, let alone 1,000, new WWW sites a day to see if anything new is of use. Luckily, many services monitor or index new sites so you can find specific resources when you need them. The bad news is that these competing search engines, directories, and databases of pointers do not *organize* resources they report on in a consistent or unified way. In addition, none of these can be considered truly comprehensive, especially since most rely on each site's administrator to notify them of the site's existence and content. Even spider-based search engines, such as Webcrawler, that regularly query servers for information about files may miss a new site if it is not reported to them. The point is that while these WWW directories and search tools provide an essential service, no single tool provides the final word on what is available on the WWW. You may want to develop a routine of checking several of the most important directories and using multiple search tools when looking for specific information.

It is also a good idea to check in about once a week with key services offering "what's new" information to monitor new resources and gather "bookmarks" for your personal reference file. Some of the best are:

- *Yahoo.* Now a commercial service, this directory was started by two Stanford University students. It is at

  www.yahoo.com (Choose "What's New" from the menu.)

- *Mosaic What's New.* This is a heavily trafficked site with subject categories different from those of Yahoo.

  http://www.ncsa.uiuc.edu/SDG/Software/Mosaic/Docs/whats-new.html

- *EINet Galaxy.* Locate it at

  http://galaxy.einet.net/galaxy.html

- *What's New Too.* Locate it at

  http://newtoo.manifest.com/WhatsNewToo/index.html

- *NCSA/GNN What's New.* This is now part of America Online. Locate it at

  http://www.gnn.com/gnn/wm/whats-new.html

Another good place to check is the Usenet newsgroup

comp.infosystems.www.announce

because many new WWW sites place their announcements there.

YANOFF LIST

Scott Yanoff is a well-known and long-time Internet guru who maintains a list known as the "Special Internet Connections" file (also called simply the Yanoff List). Yanoff's list is essentially a "best of the best" directory in a large number of subject categories, and it includes all Internet services, not just the WWW. Yanoff annotates this list, which is very helpful, and he keeps it updated. Every month or so I download it and keep it as a text file in my word processor where I can search it offline. You can get it by anonymous FTP. Enter

ftp.csd.uwm.edu

and follow the path to

/pub/inet.services.txt

Yanoff's list has also recently been made available on the WWW at

http://slacvx.slac.stanford.edu/misc/internet-services.html

ALEX: A CATALOG OF ELECTRONIC TEXTS

A few ambitious agencies, such as Project Gutenberg, are currently seeking to digitize books, especially classic literature, and make them freely available online. Digitized texts offer some important benefits for researchers in several fields, such as literary analysis. Current offerings change frequently. A regularly updated list of electronic texts is maintained at

http://www.lib.ncsu.edu/stacks/alex-index.html

INTERNET-ON-A-DISK NEWSLETTER

The Internet-on-a-Disk Newsletter, a newsletter available by E-mail, automatically sends notices of new electronic texts, including those of Project Gutenberg. To be added to the distribution list, send an E-mail message to

samizdat@world.std.com

SCOTT'S HOTLIST (SUBJECT GUIDE)

Scott's Hotlist is an excellent and very large annotated list of Internet-wide resources by subject; see it on the WWW at

http://www.picosof.com:8080/html/scott.html

When you log in to read newsgroups, you are often asked if you want to see new groups that were added since you last logged in. Sometimes this number can be very large; more than 3,000 new Usenet newsgroups have been added since I started writing this book. Still, newsgroup reader software makes it fairly simple to keep up with newly added groups by allowing you to browse in this way. It is a bit harder to keep up to date with the range of mailing lists (Listservs). One of the ways I do this is by downloading at regular intervals two moderated lists that track mailing list additions. Again, I download these lists to my word processor so that I can search the list by keywords whenever I want. The two lists that I download and their differences are:

- *The SRI List of Lists*: This is the larger of the two lists, and it is the most comprehensive. At about 1.5 megabytes it takes a while to download, and how long depends on your modem speed. It can be retrieved by anonymous FTP at

  ftp.nisc.sri.com
  path: /netinfo/interest-groups.Z

  Note that the file is compressed and must be uncompressed before you can use it.

- *Publicly Accessible Mailing Lists*: This list is available by anonymous FTP at

  rtfm.mit.edu
  Path: /pub/usenet/news.answers/mail/mailing-lists

INTERNET MONTHLY REPORT

The Internet Monthly Report is a monthly newsletter that reports on Internet statistics, trends, and other network issues. It is available in the following ways:

- By FTP. Enter

  venera.isi.edu

- By E-mail. Ask to be added to the distribution list by sending an E-mail message to

  imr-request@isi.edu

Final Considerations: How to Protect Yourself from Online Hazards

As you are no doubt aware there are hazards online. Computer viruses can crash or badly damage your computer system, destroying all your hard work. Crackers can steal personal information and use it to harm you. As businesses move online, there will be even more incentives for criminals. It is important to be aware of online dangers and take steps to protect yourself.

VIRUSES

Computer viruses are pieces of programming code designed to perform certain tasks, such as attaching to files you might download and then erasing other needed files on your local system. Some can do a lot of damage, and there are thousands of them. A constant stream of new and ever more sophisticated viruses is released every day. Because of this, it is important to protect yourself as follows:

- Get and use a software program such as McAfee's VirusScan, which is shareware and can be found on most of the FTP software repositories under directories such as VIRUS or SECURITY. You need to run the program each time you introduce new software or files from "foreign" sources, and you need to download updated versions as soon as they are available. Updated virus scanners contain ways to detect the most recent types of viruses. Other virus checkers are made by Norton Utilities and PC Tools, and the most recent version of MS-DOS also contains a virus-scanning program. Note that commercial software is a bit less effective than programs like McAfee's simply because it is not updated as often.

- Realize that viruses are usually a problem in "executable" program files (files with extensions such as .exe or .com). If you are merely reading E-mail, a newsgroup, or browsing the WWW without downloading a program, you are in no danger of "catching" a virus. Still, run your virus scanner regularly as part of preventive maintenance.

CRACKERS AND UNAUTHORIZED USE

Crackers are technically sophisticated computer users who seek to breach the security of other computers and networks for personal gain. They are a particular problem for system administrators, who must deal with a legacy of security holes left by the original **TCP/IP** developers. System administrators design elaborate measures, such as "firewalls" that cordon off parts of a machine from public access, to prevent crackers from entering their systems. Other methods include installing special software that tracks the activities of users with certain profiles, such as those who attempt to log in repeatedly with multiple, unrelated passwords. Crackers are sometimes looking for information they can exploit, such as credit card numbers. For this reason, do *not* leave files with personal or sensitive information in your online account directories. In addition, make it more difficult for crackers to use your account to illegally access the system by doing the following:

- Choose a password that is difficult for anyone else to guess. The best passwords are alphanumeric, meaning they contain both numbers and letters in a string. Avoid using your name or other words that might be easily associated with you.

- Change your password often.

- When you log on, pay attention to the message that reads "Last failed attempt" xxxxdatexxxx. This message is there to alert you to possible attempts by unauthorized users to access your account. Look at this message each time you log in. If there are failed attempts that do not represent a log-in failure you caused by a typing error or other problem, report it to your system administrator.

Putting It All Together: Harnessing the Total Internet

The Internet is now an *environment* for many people, where we can work, play, socialize, and shop. While no book or expert can say what the Internet will be like in ten years (or even next year), it is fairly certain that the Internet, or the more advanced network that replaces it, will continue to grow and become more integrated with our daily lives. Teaching you the rules of the road, how to use the tools, and what to do with them, as well as how to keep current, are the goals of this book. Putting all of these skills together should enhance your overall productivity and increase your future prospects.

I am very interested in creative ways for using the Internet that have been developed by readers of this book. Share your success stories with me at

charris@cts.com

or in care of the publisher of this book. Best wishes on your Internet explorations!

5

Glossary

56K line A high-speed, digital phone-line connection, usually a dedicated leased line, which can carry up to 56,000 bits per second (bps). It is roughly four times faster than a 14,400 bps modem. *See also* Bandwidth, Leased line, and T-1.

Acceptable Use Policy (AUP) A policy statement developed by an organization to inform users of its expectations and their responsibilities. The Internet has its own AUPs, and each Internet access provider adds its own AUPs to govern user behavior.

Acronyms Accepted Internet shorthand for various terms and expressions. For example, IMHO (In My Humble Opinion) and OTOH (On the Other Hand). *See also* Emoticons.

Agents *See* Smart Agents.

Archie A software tool for finding files stored on anonymous FTP sites. A weakness of Archie is that the user must know the exact file name or be able to define a substring of the filename because either most servers do not allow file descriptions or the original file contributors did not provide them.

Anonymous FTP   *See* FTP.

ARPA or ARPAnet (Advanced Research Projects Administration Network)   The precursor to the Internet. It was developed in the late 1960s and early 1970s by the U.S. Department of Defense as an experiment in wide-area networking that would provide secure communications in the event of a nuclear war. *See also* Internet.

ASCII (American Standard Code for Information Interchange)   The worldwide standard for the code numbers used by computers to represent a universal character set (all the upper and lowercase Latin letters, numbers, punctuation, etc.). There are 128 standard ASCII codes, each of which can be represented by a 7-digit binary number: 0000000 through 1111111.

Backbone   A high-speed line or series of connections that forms a major pathway within a network. The term is relative because a backbone in a small network is likely to be much slower than many nonbackbone lines in a large network.

Bandwidth   A term borrowed from radio terminology. In computer science it refers to speed. The amount of data that can be sent through a connection is measured by "bandwidth," usually measured in bits per second. One of the primary technical issues when considering the future of the Internet is the limit of the current bandwidth, such as that offered by the residential telephone system, which can carry at most roughly 28,000 bits per second, compared to the cable television wiring, which can carry 10,000,000 bits per second. To realize the full multimedia capabilities of the WWW, for instance, or to enjoy such features as real-time video conferencing, substantially more bandwidth must be made commonly available. Full-motion, full-screen video requires roughly 10,000,000 bits per second, depending on compression. *See also* 56K line, Bit, and T-1.

Bit (Binary digIT)   A single-digit number in base 2. In other words, either a 1 or a 0. The smallest unit of computerized data. Bandwidths are usually measured in bits per second (bps). *See also* Bandwidth, Byte, Kilobyte, and Megabyte.

BITNET (Thought to stand for "Because It's Time Network")   A network of primarily educational sites, co-existing with the Internet but separate from it. E-mail has been freely exchanged between the two networks for quite some time. However, more and more BITNET networks are moving to the Internet.

Browser   A client software program used to examine various kinds of Internet resources, such as the WWW. *See also* Client, URL, and WWW.

Byte   A set of bits that represents a single character. Usually there are 8 or 10 bits in a byte, depending on how the measurement is being made.

Cancelbot   Software that monitors activity on an Internet service and "cancels" messages sent to the server if the messages meet the criteria of the cancelbot. For example, IRC conferences sometimes attracted cancelbots developed by users who wanted to prevent others from expressing certain opinions. Sometimes they targeted the participation of a single user. Most IRC servers now ban cancelbots in any form. *See also* Cancelmoose and IRC.

Cancelmoose A piece of software written by an unknown hacker; intended to discourage spamming activities within the Usenet hierarchies. The Cancelmoose monitors worldwide Usenet posts and automatically cancels messages if the software (and/or the Cancelmoose author) detects that a single message is being sent to multiple groups simultaneously. The threshold for the number of simultaneous messages that the Cancelmoose will tolerate before canceling is unknown. *See also* Cancelbot, Spamming, and Usenet.

Client A software program that is used to obtain data from a server software program on a remote computer. *See also* Server.

Clipper Chip An onboard-chip intended to be part of an encryption scheme proposed by the U.S. government. The Clipper Chip would allow the government to decrypt any encrypted message, even those sent between private individuals. The Clipper Chip has been vehemently opposed by the Internet community as well as by foreign governments because of its potential threat to privacy and security. *See also* Digital vapor trail and Encryption.

Cracker An individual who breaks into computers to steal information or otherwise use the network for illegal or criminal activities. Crackers are distinct from hackers, who are technically advanced computer users who experiment with computers and are primarily interested in advancing knowledge about computers and their capabilities.

Cyberspace Term originated by author William Gibson in his novel *Neuromancer*. The word cyberspace is currently used to describe the overall online environment and the resources available there.

Digital vapor trail A trail or "footprint." On the Internet, user activities leave digital vapor trails or footprints so that it is possible to trace those activities. This aspect of networked computerization has led to intensified interest in computer privacy, security, and encryption. *See also* Clipper Chip and Encryption.

Domain name The unique name that identifies an Internet site. Domain names always have at least two parts separated by a period. They are best read left to right. The part on the left is the most specific, and the part on the right is more general. Usually, all of the machines on a given network will share the same domain names to the right of the last period: e.g., *microsoft.com*. There are also domain types, designated by the name to the right of the last period: com (commercial), edu (educational), net (network), etc. *See also* IP address.

E-mail (electronic mail) Messages, usually text only but possibly containing files and other data, sent from one person to another via computer. E-mail can also be sent automatically to a large number of addresses, as in the discussion groups Listserv. One of the problems with the proliferation of E-mail is that it is a "flat" communication medium, in which the emotive dimension of most human communication tends to be lost. Various methods have been used to combat this problem, such as the widespread use of emoticons. *See also* Emoticons and Listserv.

Emoticons   Pictorial characters produced with a standard computer keyboard used to express emotion or provide context in an E-mail or text message. For example, :-) conveys a smile. *See also* E-mail.

Encryption   A method of taking a message or file and scrambling the contents so that it cannot be intercepted and read by others during data transfer. Decryption is the process of undoing the scrambling (returning the message to its original form) using a keycode. Data privacy and security are important issues on the Internet, and there have been many experiments with secure encryption, such as Phil Zimmerman's PGP (Pretty Good Privacy) software. Commercial interests are keenly interested in encryption so that financial information (banking data, credit card numbers, and other transaction information) can be sent over public lines. The U.S. government is also concerned about the implementation of encryption and has offered a compromise technology in the form of the Clipper Chip. It is believed that multiple encryption schemes will emerge for common business use over the Internet in 1996 and 1997. *See also* Clipper Chip and Digital vapor trail.

Ethernet   A common method of networking computers in a local area network (LAN). Ethernet can handle about 10,000,000 bits per second and can be used with almost any kind of computer. *See also* Bandwidth and LAN.

FAQs (Frequently Asked Questions)   Documents that list and answer the most common questions on a particular subject. FAQs are provided on thousands of subjects throughout the Internet and should be read by those who wish to participate in a particular Usenet or Listserv discussion. FAQs are usually written by leaders within a Usenet, Listserv, or other discussion group. They provide the material to orient new users and relieve them from repeatedly answering the same questions.

Finger   An Internet software tool for locating people at other Internet sites. Another use is to check to see whether another user is logged on at his or her site at a particular time in order to facilitate online conferencing or chat sessions.

Flame   A negative or even nasty E-mail response, usually to a message or posting to a discussion list. Flames are a common way for the Internet community to express disapproval. *See also* Mailbombing and Spamming.

Flame war   A widespread episode of sending flames (flaming), in which flames are exchanged and the friction between parties escalates. *See also* Mailbombing and Spamming.

FTP (File Transfer Protocol)   A common method of moving files between two Internet sites. FTP is a special way to log in to another Internet site for the purposes of retrieving and/or sending files. There are thousands, perhaps millions, of Internet sites that have established publicly accessible repositories of material that can be obtained using FTP, by logging in using the account name anonymous" plus a password consisting of one's own Internet address. These sites are called "anonymous FTP servers." Many FTP sites contain shareware software, documents, or databases intended to be publicly shared.

Gopher   A method of making documents and other materials available over the Internet. It permits easy navigation by relatively transparent "tunneling" into directory/file structures. Gopher requires that the user have a Gopher client program, either through a shell or SLIP/PPP account. However, the WWW (World Wide Web) has grown more rapidly than Gopher over the last several years as a means of document delivery and navigation. *See also* Client, Hypertext, Server, and WWW.

GUI (Graphical User Interface)   Software application that allows the use of graphics, such as icons, to aid in user navigation.

Host   Any computer on a network that is a repository for services available to other computers on the network. Hosts frequently perform several services rather than being dedicated to just one. *See also* Network and Node.

HTML (HyperText Markup Language)   The programming language used to create Hypertext documents for use on the World Wide Web (WWW). *See also* HTTP, Hypertext, Mosaic, and WWW.

HTTP (HyperText Transport Protocol)   The protocol for moving Hypertext files across the Internet. It requires an HTTP client on one end and an HTTP server program on the other end. *See also* Client, Server, and WWW.

Hypertext   Generally, any text that contains "links" to other documents or resources. When chosen those materials can be retrieved and displayed, even if they reside on a remote server. Hypertext navigation is one of the primary qualities of the WWW. *See also* WWW.

Information superhighway   Words widely used to describe the coming networked society. However, many experts feel this is an unfortunate metaphor because the Internet is currently not centrally organized and lacks such highway basics as road signs, mile markers, and maps.

Internet   A worldwide network of networks.

IP (Internet Protocol address)   A unique address consisting of four parts separated by periods: for example, 189.132.2.1. Each computer on the Internet has a unique IP address. *See also* Internet.

IRC (Internet Relay Chat)   Interactive real-time discussions on servers around the world. Anyone can connect to an IRC server and start a new "channel" (a topic for discussion) or join an existing one. *See also* Cancelmoose.

ISDN (Integrated Services Digital Network)   An alternate method of moving data over existing regular phone lines. ISDN has been available to corporate customers for some time in many areas of the United States, but it has only recently become available and affordable for residential telephone customers in a few pilot programs. It can provide speeds of 64,000 bits per second over a regular phone line, but it is still not fast enough to carry video. *See also* Bandwidth and T-1.

Kilobyte   A thousand bytes. *See also* Bit and Byte.

LAN (Local Area Network)   A computer network limited to a particular area, such as within a company, a building, or department. *See also* WAN.

Leased line   A phone line that is rented for exclusive 24-hour, 7-day-a-week use from your location to another location. The highest speed data connections require a leased line. *See also* 56K line and T-1.

Listserv   The most common kind of mailing list. Many thousands are currently in existence on almost every imaginable topic. Mail is sent to a common address and copies are distributed to subscribers. Listservs are also often called "private discussion lists" because they are frequently moderated and subscription requests must be approved by either the moderator or the Listserv software. These discussions are interactive but not "real time." *See also* E-mail and Mailing list.

Lofting   Amorous online adventure. Courtship, "virtual dating," fantasy role-playing, and even online marriage are aspects of lofting.

Login   (noun) The account name used to gain access to a computer system. *See also* Password. You **log in** (verb) to a computer system.

Lurking   Joining a discussion group or IRC channel and monitoring it without participating in the discussion.

Mailbombing   A retaliatory technique, often part of a flame war, in which so much E-mail is sent to an individual user's mailbox that it causes a system crash. *See also* Flame, Flame war, and Spamming.

Mailing list   A system that allows people to send electronic mail messages to a central address. The server at this address then copies the message and sends it to all other subscribers on the mailing list. *See also* Listserv.

Megabyte   A million bytes; a thousand kilobytes. *See also* Bit, Byte, and Kilobyte.

Modem (MOdulator, DEModulator)   An internal or external device that communicates between a computer and a phone line. A modem allows the computer to talk to other computers through the phone system. Modems are rated according to how much data can be carried per second. Minimum modem speeds for Internet use are generally 14,400 bits per second (bps) or 28,800 bps, particularly for WWW access, because WWW graphics and multimedia require high speeds.

MOO (MUD, Object Oriented)   One of several kinds of multi-user role-playing environments, so far primarily text-based with limited graphic capabilities. *See also* MUD.

Mosaic   The original WWW browser or client software often credited with making the WWW viable as an Internet service. Mosaic permits the user to access the WWW with GUI (graphic user interface) capability. Until challenged by Netscape, it was the dominant and most widespread WWW browser. *See also* Browser, Client, and WWW.

MUD (Multi-User Dungeon or Domain)   A multi-user simulation environment. Some are purely recreational; others are used for serious software development or education purposes (such as online courses, presentations, or conferencing). A significant feature of most MUDs is that users can create objects or resources that remain in the space for other users and with which other users can interact in their absence, thus allowing a rich and diverse "world" to be built gradually and collectively. *See also* MOO.

Netiquette   Network etiquette. Accepted guidelines for participation in the Internet community, including social behaviors as well as technical protocols.

Network   Two or more computers connected for resource sharing. When two or more *network*s are connected an internet is created. *See also* Internet.

Newbie   A term referring to a new Internet user.

Newsgroups   The name for discussion groups on Usenet. *See also* Usenet.

Node   Any single computer connected to a network. *See also* Internet and Network.

Packet switching   A method that maximizes the efficiency of data transfer routes used to move data around on the Internet. It was an important feature in the military's vision of the Internet as a secure communications system because files and messages are never transported intact. In packet switching, a file or message to be transferred is broken up into pieces (called packets). Each packet has imprinted on it the addresses it came from and where it is going. This enables data from many different sources to share the same phone lines and to be sorted and directed to different routes by special machines along the way (routers). *See also* Router.

Password   A code used to gain access to a protected computer system. Passwords must be unique and should also resist the cracking of your account by unauthorized users. The best passwords are alphanumeric (contain letters and numbers in a string) and are not words that might easily be associated with you, such as birthdates, names of pets or significant others, or your name.

POP (Point of Presence or Post Office Protocol)   Point of presence usually means a city or location to which a network can be connected, often with dial-up phone lines. Post office protocol refers to the way E-mail software, such as Eudora, gets mail from a mail server. When you obtain a SLIP/PPP or shell account you usually get a POP account with it, and it is this POP account that Eudora (or other E-mail software) checks to handle incoming and outgoing mail. E-mail software will not work without being properly configured for your specific POP account. *See also* PPP and SLIP.

PPP (Point-to-Point Protocol)   A protocol that allows a computer to use a regular telephone line and a modem to make a TCP/IP connection to the Internet. PPP is gradually replacing SLIP for this purpose. *See also* Internet, IP address, SLIP, and TCP/IP.

Probability sampling   A sample in which every member of the population has an equal chance of being selected (also known as random sampling).

This method is necessary if the resulting sample is to be representative of the population from which it was drawn—which is necessary if you want to make generalizations or predictions based on the data.

RFCs (Request For Comments)   Documents available online that "request comments" from users concerning new proposed standards by the Internet Engineering Task Force, a consensus-building body. When standards are established, the RFC remains to document the standard. RFCs are an excellent resource for detailed technical information and background on almost every aspect of the Internet.

Router   A special-purpose computer (or software) that handles the connection between two or more networks. Routers look at the destination addresses of the packets passing through them and decide which route is best for a transfer given the characteristics of the packet and its destination. *See also* Network and Packet switching.

Server   A computer (or a software package) that provides a specific kind of service to client software running on other computers. The term can refer to a particular piece of software, such as a WWW server, or to the machine on which the software is running: for example, "Our mail server is down today, that's why E-mail is not being delivered." *See also* Client and Network.

SLIP (Serial Line Interface Protocol)   A standard for using a regular telephone line (a serial line) and a modem to connect a computer as an Internet site using the TCP/IP networking standard. SLIP is gradually being replaced by PPP. *See also* Internet, PPP, and TCP/IP.

Smart agent   Software with certain artificial intelligence capabilities that can perform customized work for a user given basic profiles, guidelines, or other information. Smart agent software is expected to be commercially available sometime in 1996. The MIT Media Lab has been active in developing smart agent software, as have many private software companies. One use of a smart agent might be to pull together a daily custom newspaper or to search for specific information.

Spamming   The practice of using the Internet to broadcast unsolicited messages. It usually results in intensive flame wars as well as other consequences, such as having the spammer's Internet access revoked. *See also* Flame and Flame war.

Surf   To navigate through the Internet, often serendipitously, looking for new sites and information. Surfing seems an appropriate metaphor for the experience of moving seamlessly from site to site, from country to country, via the hypertext links made possible by the WWW. *See also* Hypertext.

T-1   A special leased-line connection capable of carrying large amounts of data (roughly at 1,544,000 bits per second). Large businesses and corporations typically have their own T-1 lines. A T-1 line can move a megabyte in less than 10 seconds in a best-case scenario. However, that is still not fast enough for full-screen, full-motion video, with no dropped frames, for which you need at least 10,000,000 bits per second. T-1 is the fastest speed commonly used to connect networks to the Internet. *See also* 56K line, Bandwidth, Bit, Byte, and Ethernet.

TCP/IP (Transmission Control Protocol/Internet Protocol)   The suite of protocols that defines the Internet. Originally designed for the UNIX operating system, TCP/IP software is now available for every major kind of computer operating system and is routinely built into many systems today. *See also* Internet, IP address, and UNIX.

Telnet   The protocol that permits a user to log in to a remote site and use the resources there as though he or she were on site.

Terminal   A device that allows you to send commands to a computer somewhere else. At a minimum, this means a keyboard and a display screen. When connecting to the Internet or other online services, the user is frequently asked to choose a "terminal emulation" standard, which means that software will be used to "fool" the other computer into treating your computer as though it were a terminal on its own system.

UNIX   A computer operating system and platform that coordinates the activities of different software applications and the features running on "top" of it. UNIX is designed to be used by many people at the same time and to "multitask" (perform multiple activities), and it also has TCP/IP built in. It is the most common operating system for Internet servers, particularly WWW servers.

URL (Uniform Resource Locator)   The standard way to give the address of any resource on the Internet. A URL specifies the type of resource and its location, as in

gopher://gopher.umass.edu/policies/policy.doc

This URL indicates that the type of resource is a Gopher server that resides at the University of Massachusetts (umass.edu), and that the document we want *(policy.doc)* is in a directory called *policies* on this server.

A WWW URL might look like

http://www.microsoft.com/homepage.html

Here *http* specifies a WWW resource. The *.html* tag at the end of the URL also indicates that it is a WWW document. *See also* Browser, HTML, HTTP, and WWW.

Usenet   A worldwide system of discussion groups, with messages shared among hundreds of thousands of networked computers and millions of participants. Usenet consists of more than 10,000 discussion areas, called newsgroups, covering virtually every imaginable topic. Usenet is organized into topical hierarchies, such as .biz (business topics), .alt (alternative), .bio (biology), .sci (scientific), etc.

Veronica (Very Easy Rodent Oriented Network Index to Computerized Archives)   A powerful and continually updated database of the names of almost every menu item on many thousands of Gopher servers. It was developed at the University of Nevada. The Veronica database can be searched from most major Gopher menus. *See also* Gopher.

Virtual reality   Computer simulations that use 3-D graphics and devices such as special gloves, eyewear, or helmets to allow users to interact with the simulation. When virtual reality simulations improve, it will be possible to have the strong impression of physically walking through a room, seeing and talking to another person, or performing tasks such as driving a car or an airplane while you are online. Virtual reality (also referred to as VR) will also have implications for medicine (remote telemedicine and virtual surgery), education (the virtual classroom), and the workplace (the virtual worker). *See also* Cyberspace.

WAIS (Wide Area Information Servers)   A commercial software package that allows the indexing of huge quantities of information and also provides a searchable interface to those indices. WAIS is available on various servers around the Internet and can also be downloaded as a client shareware package for SLIP/PPP accounts.

WAN (Wide Area Network)   Any internet or network that covers an area larger than a single building or cluster of buildings, such as an office park or university campus. Thus remote offices connected to an organization's network are usually connected as part of a WAN. *See also* Internet, LAN, and Network.

WWW (World Wide Web)   The universe of hypertext servers (HTTP servers) that allow text, graphics, sound, and other multimedia files to be viewed together and navigated via hypertext links. The WWW and its browser software packages (such as Mosaic, Netscape, and Lynx) also provide a user friendly front end to such Internet features as FTP, Gopher, Usenet, Messaging (E-mail), and WAIS. *See also* Browser, FTP, Gopher, HTTP, Telnet, and WAIS.

References

Abernathy, J. (1994, May). Highway Robbery: Selling the Net. *PC World*, pp. 56–66.

ABI and YellowNet Partner on Internet Listings. (1995, April 26). *Cowles/Simba Media Daily*.

Adam, J. A. (1994, September). Roundtable Debate: Upgrading the Information Infrastructure. *IEEE Spectrum*, pp. 22–29.

Alexander, M. (1991, April 29). Hackers Find Open Season on Internet. *Computerworld*, p. 8.

Angell, D., & Heslop, B. (1994). *The Elements of E-mail Style: Communicate Effectively via Electronic Mail*. Addison-Wesley Publishing Company.

Anthes, G. H. (1991, August 5). Internet Society to Guide Research Net. *Computerworld*, p. 42.

Anthes, G. H. (1994, January 17). EPA Gives Public Free Access to Its Data. *Computerworld*, p. 41.

Armstrong, C. A., J.A. (1988). *Manual of Online Search Strategies*. G. K. Hall & Company.

Arndt, M. (1994, July 22). Census: College Cost Is High; So Is Payoff. *San Diego Union Tribune*, pp. A1 & A10.

Associated Press. (1994, July 22). Hackers Invade Pentagon Link, Filch Nonsecret Computer Data. *San Diego Union Tribune*, p. A5.

Aware, the Boys Are. (1995, March). *NetGuide*, p. 25.

Baker, N. (1994, April 4). Annals of Scholarship: Discards. *The New Yorker*, pp. 64–86.

Baldwin, D. (1994, Spring). If This Is the Information Superhighway, Where Are the Rest Stops? *Common Cause Magazine*, pp. 17–23.

Barlow Close, D. (1994, June). Quick Tips. *Internet World*, pp. 16–17.

Barlow, J. P. (1994, February 9). Jackboots on the Infobahn. *Wired*, pp. 20–22.

Barrett, T. A. (1994, November/December). Virtual Encounters. *Internet World*, p. 45.

Berry, J. N., III. (1993, October 1). We Need Some Cyberspace: Don't Turn the Information Superhighway into a Supermarket. *Library Journal*, p. 6.

Betts, M. (1994, January 31). Critics Anticipate Privacy Abuses on Superhighway. *Computerworld*, p. 27.

Blystone, K. (1993, August 20). Building a School without Buildings. *Electronic Journal of Virtual Culture*.

Browning, G. (1993, December 4). Dueling over Data. *National Journal*, pp. 2880–2884.

Calcari, S. (1994, September). A Snapshot of the Internet. *Internet World*, pp. 54–58.

Cerone, D. (1994, April 17). Hollywood On-Line. *Los Angeles Times*, pp. 7, 82–83.

Chang, R. (1994, September 8). Purchase to Speed Up TV Home Shopping Mall. *San Diego Union Tribune*, pp. A1 & C2.

Civets, K. (1994, June). E-mail Tricks. *Internet World*, pp. 39–42.

Civets, K. M. (1994, September). Digital Lit. *Internet World*, pp. 86–88.

Clari.nb.trends. (1994, April). Denmark Ready for Cashless Revolution. *The Clari News*, p. 1.

Clark, A. (1994, September). NASA in Cyberspace. *Internet World*, pp. 44–47.

Clement, G. P. (1994, September). Library without Walls. *Internet World*, pp. 60–64.

Clement, G. P. (1994, June). There's Something for Everyone on the Internet. *Internet World*, pp. 35–37.

The Complete Survival Guide to the Information Superhighway. (1994, May). *Popular Science*, p. 35.

Computer Ethics Statement. (1993, June). *College & Research Libraries News*, pp. 331–332.

Content Online & Interactive Services Monthly. (1994, April).

Crawley, J. (1994, July 19). He Puts the 'Info' in 'Info Superhighway.' *Computerlink*, p. 7.

Crawley, J. W. (1994, August 16). Internet Can Come Cheap If You Have the Right Number. *Computerlink*, pp. 1 & 10.

Cronin, M. J. (1993, December). Internet Business Resources. *Database*, pp. 47–54.

Cronin, M. J. (1993, December 6). Internet Shortcuts. *Computerworld*, p. 63.

Cronin, M. J. (1994, August). Where to Go on the Internet. *Home Office Computing*, p. 54.

Cybercriminals Beware! (1994, October). *Medea Magazine*, p. 36.

Davidow, W. H., & Malone, M. (1992). *The Virtual Corporation*. Harper Business.

Dean, D. (1994, June). Internet Bookshelf. *Internet World*, p. 92.

Dennis, E. E. (1994, May). Tracking the Coming of the Information Superhighway. *American Journalism Review*, p. S2.

Dern, D. P. (1994, September). .GIFs at 11: The Many Deaths of the Internet. *Internet World*, pp. 99–101.

Deutsch, P. (1994, September). The Ten Commandments of the Internet. *Internet World*, pp. 96–98.

Digital Connections: Kids and the Future. (1994, November). *Medea Magazine*, p. 40.

Diller, B. (1995, February). Don't Repackage, Redefine. *Wired*, pp. 82–84.

Duderstadt, H. (1995, February). Advertising in the Digital Domain. *Medea Magazine*, pp. 20–21.

Eagan, A. (1993, December). Order Out of Chaos: Science Databases on the Internet. *Database*, pp. 62–68.

Eddy, A. (1994). *Internet After Hours*. Prima.

Edwards, H. C. (1994, July/August). Getting Wired. *Aldus Magazine*, pp. 36–39.

Ellsworth, J. H., & Ellsworth, M. V. (1994). *The Internet Business Book*. John Wiley & Sons, Inc.

Farhi, P., & Sugawara, S. (1993, December 19). Will The Information Superhighway Detour the Poor? *Washington Post*, p. H1.

Feinberg, A. (1990). Netiquette. *Lotus 6, 9*, 66–69.

Fitzgerald, K. (1994, February 14). Info Wish List. *Advertising Age*, p. 119.

Fraase, M. (1994). *The Windows Internet Tour Guide Cruising The Internet The Easy Way*. Ventana Press, Inc.

Furger, R. (1994, September). Unequal Distribution: The Information Haves and Have-Nots. *PC World*, p. 30.

Galloway, T. (1994, June). Are You Really . . . ? *Internet World*, pp. 52–55.

Gans, H. J. (1994, Winter). The Electronic Shut-ins: Some Social Flaws of the Information Superhighway. *Media Studies Journal*, pp. 123–129.

Germain, J. M. (1994, April 22). Love and Marriage On Line. *ComputerEdge*, pp. 14–15.

Gilliam, D. (1994, March 19). Getting on Today's Road to Freedom. Washington *Post*, p. B1.

Gillmor, D. (1994, June). A Journalist's View of the Internet. *Internet World*, pp. 31–33.

Godin, S. (1994). *E-Mail Addresses of the Rich and Famous*. Seth Godin Productions, Inc.

Godwin, M. (1994, September). Government Eavesdropping. *Internet World*, pp. 93–95.

Godwin, M. (1994, June). Libel, Public Figures, and The Net. *Internet World*, pp. 62–64.

Gold, J. (1994, May 1). Working It Out. *Los Angeles Times Magazine*, p. 10.

Goldberg, F. S. (1988, May). Telecommunications and the Classroom: Where We've Been and Where We're Going. *The Computing Teacher*, pp. 26–30.

Goldman, N. (1992). *Online Information Hunting*. Windcrest/McGraw-Hill.

Gomery, D. (1994, Summer). In Search of the Cybermarket. *Wiring America*, pp. 9–17.

Goode, J., & Johnson, M. (1991, November). Putting Out the Flames: The Etiquette and Law of E-Mail. *Online*, pp. 61–65.

Gore, A. J. (1994, January 20). Gore Unveils Plans For 'Information Superhighway.' *Facts on File*, p. 32.

Gotterbarn, D. (1991, Summer). Computer Ethics: Responsibility Regained. *National Forum*, pp. 26–31.

Graham, F. (1994, October). Sam's Dream Programs. *Newmedia*, p. 16.

Greenberg, K. (1994, June). Caution! I Brake for FTP Sites! *Internet World*, pp. 78–79.

Greenberg, K. (1994, September). The Art of the Internet. *Internet World*, pp. 102–103.

Groves, M. (1994, May 18). Lotus Founder Working to Guard Privacy in the Electronic Age. *Los Angeles Times*, p. B9.

Gruener, G. (1994, September). Go On-line, Young Man. *Internet World*, p. 48.

A Guide for Accessing California Legislative Information over Internet. (1994). Legislative Counsel Bureau, State of California.

Hafner, K. (1994, December 5). The MBone: Can't You Hear It Knocking? *Newsweek*, p. 86.

Hahn, H., & Murdock, W. (1994, September). Net.Imperative. *Boardwatch*, pp. 66–69.

Hahn, H., & Stout, R. (1994). *The Internet Yellow Pages*. Osborne McGraw-Hill.

Hancock, L. (1995, February 27). The Haves and the Have Nots. *Newsweek*, pp. 50–53.

Harmon, A. (1994, Saturday May 7). Last Off-Ramp on Information Highway. *Los Angeles Times*, pp. v113, D2.

Harrah Cady, G. (1994, June). Life in the Fast Lane: A Day in the Life of an Internet Consultant. *Internet World*, pp. 80–82.

Harris, C. (1995, Fall, forthcoming). Survey Research and the Internet. *Electronic Journal of Virtual Culture*. (htpp://www.marshall.edu/vstepp/vri/ejvc/ejvc.html)

Hauptman, R. (1991, Fall). Ethics and the Dissemination of Information. *Library Trends*, pp. 199–375.

Heilbrunn, H. (1994, August 22). More Potholes on the I-Way. *Mediaweek*, p. 16.

Heim, J. (1993, November). Communications Q&A. *PC World*, p. 332.

Heim, J. (1994, April). Communications Q&A. *PC World*, p. 290.

Herbert, J. (1995, March). Mega Connections and Other Questions. *Medea Magazine*, pp. 18–19.

Hill, M. R. (1993). *Archival Strategies and Techniques*. SAGE Publications.

Hiltz, S. R. (1986, Spring). The 'Virtual Classroom': Using Computer Mediated Communication for University Teaching. *Journal of Communication*, pp. 99–104.

Horowitz, L. (1988). *Knowing Where to Look: The Ultimate Guide to Research*. Writer's Digest Books.

Hudson, R. L. (1994, April 18). Europeans Test Drive 'Smart Cards' as Key to Navigating Information Highway. *Wall Street Journal*, p. A7D.

Humphrey, D. (1995, March). Online Industry Research. *Online Access*, p. 32.

Industry Byte. (1995, March). *Online Access*, p. 17.

The Internet Letter. (1993). A Net Week Inc.

Internet News. (1994, June). *Internet World*, pp. 10–16.

Internet News. (1994, September). Smart Searches. *Internet World*, p. 10.

The Internet Unleashed. (1994). Sams Publishing.

Internet: The Undiscovered Country. (1994, March 15). *PC Magazine*, pp. 116–119.

An Interview with Apple's Errik Fair. (1994, June). *Internet World*, pp. 45–51.

Jacobs, D. (1995, January 3). Businesses Admit Snooping on Workers. *San Diego Union Tribune*, p. C4.

Jones, A., & Gill Kirkup et al. (1992). Providing Computing for Distance Learners. *Computers in Education, 18*, 183–193.

Kantor, A. (1994, September). Flame-broiled Lawyers. *Internet World*, p. 17.

Kantor, A. (1994, October). Seek and Ye Shall Find. *Internet World*, pp. 23–26.

Kantor, A., & Berlin, E. (1994, September). The Surfboard. *Internet World*, pp. 16–18.

Kantor, A., & Neubarth, M. (1994, September). The Greatest Network Story Ever Told. *Internet World*, pp. 74–75.

Kapor, M. (1991). Civil Liberties in Cyberspace. *Scientific American, 265*(3), 158–164.

Karraker, R. (1994, Spring). Making Sense of the 'Information Superhighway.' *Whole Earth Review*, pp. 18–24.

Keighron, P. (1994, June 10). Superhighway Robbery: Social and Economic Impact of the Information Superhighway. *New Statesman & Society*, p. 31.

Kelly, M. (1994, January). Mining Mathematics on the Internet. *Arithmetic Teacher*, pp. 276–282.

Klein, J. (1994, May). Government Moves Toward On-Line Procurement Process: Initiative Offers Big. *The Internet Letter*.

Kline, C. (1994). The Internet Index. *National Consultant, 4*(2).

Koch, N. (1991, November). For Writer's Block, A Writer's Bloc. *The Journal, Writers Guild of America*, pp. 24–26.

Kochmer, J. (1992). *User Services Internet Resource Guide*. NorthWest Net Academic Computing Consortium, Inc.

Kreighron, P. (1994, June 10). Super-highway Robbery. *New Statesman & Society*, p. 31.

Krol, E. (1992). *The Whole Internet: User's Guide & Catalog*. O'Reilly & Associates, Inc.

Kroll, J. (1994, July 19). Nothing Is Sacred: NSFnet Goes Capitalist. *Computerlink*, p. 3.

Kruger, P. (1994). They're Trying for Jobs the Techno Way. *San Diego Union Tribune*, p. C3.

Kushner, D. (1994, December). DragNet: Confessions of a Cyberlesbian. *Details*, p. 76.

Lambert, S., & Howe, W. (1994). *Internet Basics: Your Online Access to the Global Electronic Highway*. Random House.

Larijani, C. L. (1994). *The Virtual Reality Primer*. McGraw-Hill, Inc.

Larsen, E. (1994). *The Naked Consumer: How Our Private Lives Become Public Commodities*. Penguin Books.

Lear-Newman, E. (1994, September). Internet Blues. *Internet World*, p. 76.

Lemay, L. (1995). *Teach Yourself Web Publishing with HTML*. Sams Publishing.

Levison, A. (1993, December). Latin America Online: Best Databases For News, Business and Current Affairs. *Database*, pp. 14–27.

Li, X., & Crane, N. B. (1994). *Electronic Style: A Guide to Citing Electronic Information*. Meckler.

Lippert, P. (1994, November). Cinematic Representations of Cyberspace. Speech Communication Association (SCA). New Orleans.

Lippis, N. (1994, February 8). Ready for the Networking Channel? *PC Magazine*, p. NE41.

Locke, C. (1994, September). The Future Internet. *Internet World*, pp. 22–24.

Lohr, S. (1994). Status @sym.bol On The 'Net.'

MacKinnon, R. (1992). Searching for Leviathan in Usenet. Master's Thesis. San Jose CA: San Jose State University.

Maddox, T. (1994, Summer). The Cultural Consequences of the Information Superhighway. *Wilson Quarterly*, pp. 29–36.

Markey, E. J. (1993, February 18). Networked Communities and the Laws of Cyberspace. In *Computer Science and Telecommunications Board*. Rights and Responsibilities of Participants in Networked Communities. Washington, DC: National Research Council/Academy of Sciences.

Marton, A. (1994, March 28). Marketers: An Afterthought in Highway Construction Plans. *Brandweek*, p. 23.

Matarazzo, J., & Manshel, D. (1994, March 30). Info-highway to Nowhere. *Christian Science Monitor*, p. 22.

McAvoy, K. (1994, April 4). Infrastructure Bill's Cost: Money, FCC Staff. *Broadcasting & Cable*, p. 34.

McCahill, M. P. (1994, September). What's New with Gopher? *Internet World*, pp. 90–92.

Meeks, B. (1994, February 9). The End of Privacy. *Wired*, p. 18.

The Message in the Medium: The First Amendment on the Information Superhighway. (1994, March). *Harvard Law Review*, pp. 1062–1098.

Metcalfe, B. (1994, May 30). Advertising Can Save the Internet from Becoming a Utopia Gone Sour. *Infoworld*, p. 48.

Meyer, M. (1995, February 6). Stop! Cyberthief! *Newsweek*, p. 36.

Moody, J. (1994, September). Close-Up Telecommuting. *PC World*, p. 61.

Murray, B. (1995, February). Society, Cyberspace and the Future. Aspen Exploratory Workshop. The Markle Foundation.

Nickell, N. (1994, May 17). Internet Users 'Lock Up' Lawyers for Breach of 'Netiquette.' *The Arizona Republic*, p. D1.

Nickerson, G. (1994, January). Mining for Gold. *CD-ROM Professional*, pp. 128–132.

Noack, D. R. (1994, September). Sports on the Net. *Internet World*, pp. 81–84.

Notess, G. R. (1994, January). Telnet Explored. *Internet*, pp. 94–97.

Novak, D. (1995, January 1). Challenges of Electronic Commerce. *Wired*, p. 17.

OKeefe. (1995, February 20). [E-mail message] (Cheryl Harris, Ed.). Rensselaer Polytechnic Institute, Troy, NY.

Persson, E. (1993). *NetPower Resource Guide to Online Computer Services*. Fox Chapel Publishing.

Peterson, M. (1993, November–December). Life on the Internet: Portrait of a Collaboration. *North American Review*, pp. 10–12.

Phillips, G. M. (1994, April). The Internet: The National Information Infrastructure. *Communication Education*, pp. 73–86.

Pope, G. T. (1994, January). Bytes in the Fast Lane. *Discover*, pp. 93–96.

Powell Crowe, E. (1994). *The Electronic Traveller Exploring Alternative Online Systems*. McGraw-Hill, Inc.

Rapp, A. (1994, October). Virtual Therapy. *Newmedia*, p. 127.

Raskin, R. (1994, April 26). Why Stay off the Highway? *PC Magazine*, p. 30.

Ratzan, L. (1994, February). Everything Is Somewhere No Matter Where It Is. *Wilson Library Bulletin*, p. 60.

Reality Check. (1994, July/August). *Aldus Magazine*, p. 47.

Regan, T. (1993, Winter). Getting Health Facts from Internet. *Nieman Reports*, p. 43.

Reid, C. (1993, November 15). Writers Forum Looks at New Media, Internet. *Publishers Weekly*, p. 25.

Reno, J. (1994, June 5). Hack Attack. *Los Angeles Times Magazine*, p. 8.

Reno, J. (1994, June 5). Interface and Trouble. *Los Angeles Times Magazine*, p. 8.

Rifkin, G. (1991, October). The Ethics Gap. *Computerworld*, pp. 83–85.

Rinaldi, A. H. (1992, September 3). The Net User Guidelines and Netiquette. Unpublished paper.

Roberts, P. (1994, July/August). Techno-Talk. *Aldus Magazine*, pp. 45–50.

Rogers, G. (1989, Spring). Teaching a Psychology Course by Electronic Mail. *Social Science Computer Review*, pp. 60–64.

Rosentiel, T. B. (1994, May 18). Someone May Be Watching. *Los Angeles Times*, p. A12.

Ross, R. (1994, June). Shopping on the Information Superhighway. *PC World*, p. 59.

Rothfeder, J. (1992). *Privacy for Sale: How Computerization Has Made Everyone's Private Life an Open Secret*. Simon & Schuster.

Rowland, L. (1994, April). Libraries and Librarians on the Internet. *Communication Education*, pp. 143–150.

Rugge, S. A. (1992). *The Information Broker's Handbook*. Windcrest/McGraw-Hill.

Salus, P. (1994, September). Pioneers of the Internet. *Internet World*, pp. 70–72.

Salus, P. H. (1994, June). Net Resources: What's There and How to Approach It. *Internet World*, pp. 75–76.

Samuelson, R. J. (1993, December 16). Lost on the Information Highway. *Washington Post*, p. A.

Sandberg, J. (1993, November 23). This Information Superhighway Carries Some Very Silly Drivers. *Wall Street Journal*, p. B1.

Saunders, L. (1994, June 2). Ethics in Cyberspace. *Internet World*. Conference paper.

Savetz, K. (1994, September). Digital Lit. *Internet World*, pp. 86–88.

Schrage, M. (1995, March). Collaborative Relationships and Virtual Organizations. *Educom Review*, pp. 16–17.

Sclove, R. (1994, June 2). The Social Effects of the Internet. *Internet World*. Conference paper.

Sclove, R. E. (1994, January 12). Democratizing Technology. *The Chronicle of Higher Education*, p. B1.

Sclove, R., & Scheur, J. (1994, May 29). The Ghost in the Modem. *The Washington Post*, p. E2.

Seabrok, J. (1994, June 6). Brave New World Dept. My First Flame. *The New Yorker*, pp. 70–79.

Senechal, A. (1994, July/August). Books in Hyperspace. *Aldus Magazine*, p. 40.

Shade, L. (1994, February). Computer Supported Cooperative Work and Academic Culture. *Electronic Journal of Virtual Culture*.

Shapiro, N., & Anderson, R. (1985). Toward an Ethics and Etiquette for Electronic Mail. *Rand Document R-3283-NSF/RC, ED 169 003*.

Shermach, K. (1994). Marketing's Task: Make Ride on the Info Highway a Pleasant One. *Business Publication of the American Marketing Association, 28*(6).

Sherman, S. (1994, April 18). Will the Information Superhighway Be the Death of Retailing. *Fortune*, p. 98.

Singer, M. (1994, June 15). Superhighway a Mystery to Most. *Folio: The Magazine for Magazine Management*, p. 20.

Smith, R. J. (1991, October). The Electronic Information Course as an Alternative Teaching Method. *Research and Education Networking*, pp. 10–12.

Snyder, J. (1994, June). The Golden Age of Heroes. *Internet World*, pp. 58–59.

Soreff, Z. (1995, April). Our Brilliant Careers. *Netguide*, pp. 49–56.

Spector, M. (1994). E-mail a Godsend for Needy Russians. *The Arizona Republic*, P. E2.

Stewart, T. A. (1994, July 11). Managing in a Wired Company. *Fortune*, pp. 44–56.

Stoll, C. (1995, February 27). The Internet? Bah! *Newsweek*, p. 41.

Strangelove, M. (1994, Spring Quarter). The Essential Internet. *The Resource*, pp. 1–4.

Strangelove, M. (1994, July 21). The Geography of Consciousness. *Research on Virtual Culture*. (http://www.phoenix.ca/sie/geo-art.html)

Sugawara, S. (1994, March 14). Blue Highway. *Washington Post*, p. WB19.

Superhighway Summit: The Superhighway's Impact On The Landscape. (1994, April). *Emmy*, pp. A18–A55.

Sussman, V. (1994, January 17). Pamphleteering in the Electronic Age; Hacking Out a Digitized Proclamation of Rights. *U.S. News & World Report*, p. 55.

Taubes, G. (1994, August 12). Taking The Data in Hand—Literally—With Virtual Reality. *Science*, pp. 884–886.

Taylor, D. (1994, September). Caribbean Vacation. *Internet World*, pp. 29–31.

Taylor, R. (1994, September). Brave New Internet. *Internet World*, pp. 36–42.

Tennant, R., Ober John, & Lipow, A. G. (1993). *Crossing the Internet Threshold: An Instructional Handbook*. Library Solutions Press.

Tenner, E. (1994, Summer). Learning from the Net. *Wilson Quarterly*, pp. 18–28.

Tetzeli, R. (1994, March 7). The Internet and Your Business. *Fortune*, pp. 86–92.

Tetzeli, R. (1994, July 11). Surviving Information Overload. *Fortune*, pp. 60–65.

Tolly, K. (1994, May). Business over the Internet? Not Now, Not Ever. *Data Communications*, pp. 33–34.

Tomaiuolo, N. G. (1993, December). Internet Database Review: The FDA BBS. *Database*, pp. 82–85.

Trends & Interfaces. (1994, November). *PC World*, p. 182.

Truong, H. (1993, March). Gender Issues in Online Communications. In *3rd Annual Conference*. Computers, Freedom and Privacy. San Francisco.

Tuss, J. (1994, January). Roadmaps to the Internet: Finding the Best Guidebook for Your Needs. *Online*, p. 14.

Ubois, J. (1994, September). Present at the Creation. *Internet World*, pp. 66–69.

Uretsky, S. (1994, June). The Usenet sci.med. Newsgroups. *Internet World*, pp. 26–27.

Ventura, M. (1994, May 8). The 21st Century Is Now. *Los Angeles Times Magazine*, pp. 22–26.

Waldrop, M. M. (1994, August 12). Software Agents Prepare to Sift the Riches of Cyberspace. *Science*, pp. 882–883.

Waldrop, M. M. (1994, August 12). Culture Shock on the Networks. *Science*, pp. 879–881.

Warren, D. (1994, October). Is It Love or Is It Cybersex? *Newmedia*, p. 127.

We, G. (1994, July 26). Cross Gender Communication in Cyberspace. *Electronic Journal of Virtual Culture*. (ftp://byrd.mu.wvnet.edu/pub/ejvc/we.v2n3)

Weber, J. (1993, October 31). This Byte Is Brought to You by . . . ; Marketers are Designing 'Billboards' for Information Superhighway (Vol. 112, p. D3).

Weiss, A. (1995, April). Hop Skip and Jump. *Internet World*, p. 41.

West, D. (1994, September 12). Frank Talk about Disney and TV. *Broadcasting & Cable*, pp. 34–39.

White, M. A. (1983, May). Synthesis of Research on Electronic Learning. *Educational Leadership*, pp. 13–15.

Wiederhorn, K. (1994, May). Surfing the Internet. *The Journal*, pp. 22–25.

Wolff, M. (1994). *Netgames: Your Guide to the Games People Play on the Electronic Highway*. Random House.

Wonnacott, L., & Irvin, S. (1994, May 30). Trying to Synchronize Duplicate E-mail Names Requires Double Think. *Infoworld*, p. 65.

A World Gone Wired. (1994, August 22). *Time*, p. 24.

Wright, R. (1994, January/February). Life on the Internet. *Utne Reader*, pp. 101–109.

WWW Closes In on Top-Ranked Service. (1995, February 1). *The Internet Letter: On Corporate Users, Internetworking and Information Services*, p. 5.

INDEX